THE SPIRIT
OF INTIMACY

THE

ANCIENT
TEACHINGS
IN THE WAYS
OF
RELATIONSHIPS

SPIRIT
OF INTIMACY

SOBONFU SOMÉ

HARPER

NEW YORK • LONDON • TORONTO • SYDNEY

This book was originally published in 1997 by Berkeley Hills Books.

A hardcover edition of this book was published in 1999 by William Morrow.

THE SPRIIT OF INTIMACY. Copyright © 1997, 1999 by Sobonfu E. Somé. All rights reserved. Printed in the United States of America. No part of this book may be used or reproduced in any manner whatsoever without written permission except in the case of brief quotations embodied in critical articles and reviews. For information, address HarperCollins Publishers Inc., 195 Broadway, New York, NY 10007.

HarperCollins books may be purchased for educational, business, or sales promotional use. For information, please e-mail the Special Markets Department at SPsales@harpercollins.com.

First Quill edition published 2000.

Reprinted in Quill 2002.

Designed by Cheryl L. Cipriani

Library of Congress Cataloging-in-Publication Data is available.

ISBN 0-688-17579-1

23 24 25 26 27 LBC 34 33 32 31 30

CONTENTS

v

FOREWORD

It is an honor and pleasure to offer this foreword to *The Spirit of Intimacy*. What Sobonfu Somé has to say here reflects the wisdom of many generations of the Dagara people of West Africa. A lyrical conversation, this book invites us, as good conversations do, to wind along, dip deeply and circle back again. Taken from recorded interviews and workshops over the course of several years, it allows us to participate in storytelling, to take the circular route. This expression, which reflects Sobonfu's oral tradition of teaching, allows us a peek, a precious moment of entry into an indigenous frame of being, which is nothing without spirit, can be nothing without spirit.

This book has no theory to prove, no agenda to push, no one to impress. Sobonfu does not endeavor to fix what's broken in our relationships and marriages, and she steers clear of our one-dimensional obsession with behavioral change. What we are invited into is a living and vibrant cosmos where relations between men and women serve spirit, the community, and the ancestors. Sobonfu opens the possibility of remembering that all matters of heart are initiated by spirit, and it is to this source that our attention needs to turn when considering the health and wellness of our relationships.

Sobonfu holds in her body, in her awareness, and in her actions that which many of us in the West long for without knowing how to name. Raised in a traditional Dagara village, taught by the elders, a participant in the tribal initiation of women and the years of mentoring that follow such initiation, she is a woman who knows the depths of grief and the soaring of joy. Her intimate connection with life is so full, so abundantly rich, that to read her words is to witness deeply held truths, to awaken parts of us long ago lulled into numb acquiescence.

Her world view is in many ways vastly different from the one that is familiar to us in the West. Notions of intimacy and sexuality are frequently turned completely around from what we assume to be true. Our belief in the primacy of the individual, for example, gives rise to relationships that are "privatized," owned by us and cut off from community and from spirit. In the indigenous worldview of Sobonfu's people, the idea of a relationship existing outside the context of the village and the sacred is absurd and extremely dangerous.

We have gradually learned from Sobonfu over the last several years that marriage, indeed any relationship, is a gift from spirit and requires our gratitude and a willingness to hear what spirit has brought us together for. We have learned that here in the West, just as in Sobonfu's culture, purpose is central to existence, and relationships are avenues for one's purpose to be expressed. Intimacy is not designed or encouraged for the achievement of personal happiness; rather it is for the fulfillment of one's life purpose, for the enrichment of the village, and for the expression of spirit. It is a means of offering the gifts you carry.

These ideas are near heresy to us with our sense of entitlement, "the pursuit of happiness," but when it comes to matters of relationship, there is indeed a larger vision than we have imagined. We are culturally in our adolescence concerning intimacy. What is offered here, in these pages, are openings into an ancient culture whose wisdom can help us take the next step.

One difficulty westerners may encounter when reading Sobonfu's thoughts and ideas is that they are not always linear, building conceptually toward their conclusion. Rather, this book is a conversation, reflecting her intimacy with her land, people, and ancestors. Our addiction to information will not get fed here either, although much of what you will encounter is new and provocative. It cannot be grasped like data to be inserted into statistics and strategies. There is a word in Dagara that translates as "the thing that knowledge cannot eat." Much of what Sobonfu shares in these pages is difficult for our logical mind to grab hold of and thereby defies being another commodity for consumption. Each offering must be taken in through another faculty—the heart, soul, intuition, however you name it—and respected, nurtured, embodied.

The indigenous world from which Sobonfu speaks with authority offers us a perspective on relationships that helps restore their sacred context. She invites us into an adult stance in relationships—with our partners, with our communities, and with spirit. She offers us a mature vision and challenges us to become more of who we are. May her words simultaneously whet and quench your thirst. Drink deeply.

—JULIA AND FRANCIS WELLER
Sebastopol, California
Friends and therapists

ACKNOWLEDGMENTS

This book would never have been possible without the dedication and invaluable contribution of beings and people around me.

I would like to thank all my ancestors and spirit allies for guiding me and keeping me on my path. My respect and thanks go to the spirit of this land for welcoming and holding me. My gratitude goes to my elders and my husband for their unconditional support and input. From my heart, I thank Bernadette Smyth for her devotion in transcribing the teachings. And to all those who have helped me along the way—you know who you are—my special thanks.

I don't have this discussion of relationships all laid out, systematized, and so forth. There are all kinds of images that come in and out like stars, little stars, so you're going to have to paste these images together in order to make some sense out of them. But what is important is to look at our understanding of intimacy as primarily a practice ordered by spirit, or authorized by spirit, and executed by someone who recognizes that she cannot, by herself, make happen what she has been invited toward.

CHAPTER 1

DANO: HOME TO THE OLD WAYS

The Dagara people are mainly associated with the West African coastal countries of Ghana, Ivory Coast, and Togo. Inland from these countries, at their northern border, is Burkina Faso, formerly referred to as Upper Volta. In 1984 the government of Upper Volta decided that its colonial name was too troublesome, so they chose a new name, which means "the land of the proud ancestors."

When, in 1882, a European council sitting in Belgium tried to figure out how to share this big land of Africa, they ended up dividing the Dagara tribe into three different nations. There are a few hundred thousand Dagara people in Burkina Faso, another few hundred thousand in Ghana, and a smaller number in the Ivory Coast. This division of people occurred as a result of the arbitrary nature of colonial powers, who didn't accept tribal communities as nations.

Socially or communally, we are not that different from

indigenous communities elsewhere. Maybe what should be mentioned is that we don't have the amenities that one has here in the West, such as electricity or running water. We don't live in houses without cockroaches. We're very close to the earth and to nature, and that is the gift that we receive from such a place.

In the village, where life is directly inspired by the earth, by the trees, by the hills and rivers, the kind of relationship that exists between man and nature is directly translated in subtle ways into the building of the community and into the building of the relationships that exist between people.

When asked where they are from, the Dagara people who live in Burkina Faso usually say the village of Dano. This is because even though there are many villages in the tribe, Dano is the biggest. But it's nothing like a town by modern standards. It's just a village surrounded by other villages. It's difficult to know how many people live here, since in Africa we don't count people.

People know one another from village to village, having family and friends in many of these small communities. This comes about through marriage and immigration and through active neighborhood relationships.

In Dano the streets have no names. There is one main

street, which comes off the road that connects Dano to the main highway and Ouagadougou, the capital city. It's probably around three hundred kilometers to Ouagadougou. If you have your own car, you could probably make the drive in three and a half hours. The road out to the main highway is not paved, and it has lots of big holes, and animals and people crossing, so it can take you a long time.

Buses travel this road. They stop every ten miles or so to check in with somebody or to drop somebody off, so it's not steady travel. The thing is, no one seems to be in a hurry, so by bus it can take you a minimum of six hours to a whole day to reach the capital. That is, if you don't have any kind of mechanical breakdown.

The land is what you would call a savanna, mostly hilly grassland with few trees taller than 30 feet. The tallest tree is the baobab, which grows really high, about 180 feet. Although it's no longer forestlike, in certain places we do have dense groves of trees such as the shea, which is known for its healing power. The shea tree gives this green, delicious fruit; we eat the fruit and use the nut to make butter. The butter is used by the Dagara people for medicinal purposes, for cooking, and for cosmetics.

After you've lived, as I have, in places like Michigan or

even Northern California, the weather in Dano no longer seems so cold. But I remember when I lived there it used to be really cold. I used to think when it dropped into the seventies it was cold. Now that I've lived in a climate where the temperature might drop to thirty degrees or even lower, seventy seems pretty hot.

Even though Burkina Faso has three relatively large rivers, in the area of Dano there are only seasonal creeks and ponds. These are our sources of drinking water, and we dig wells during the dry season, which starts in November and lasts until mid-June, sometimes July. Then we have to rely only on wells for water to drink.

In the driest seasons, you will find the whole village gathered around one well of water, sometimes spending the whole night waiting for the well to fill up. This is because at these times of year the water comes at certain hours only. Very early in the morning, for example, the water table will be high. Then at noon it will be at its lowest point. We will have to go at night in order to be there when the water returns. Families with children are served first, together with pregnant women and the elderly, then everybody else is served last. So even if you have been waiting during the night, if a family with children arrives, they will be served before you.

You would call our economy agricultural, perhaps subsistence farming; we produce the food we need to live. We have not done any exporting, even though in recent years the government has been trying to get us to do so. That, to us, is a foreign concept that we have yet to learn to deal with, because we grow exactly what we need and no more.

Our main way of trading is to barter, although in the village we also use cowry shells for money as well as for divination and healing. These little white shells were brought by the Dagara people from Ghana a long time ago when the tribe used to live closer to the sea. Cowry shells are used sort of like gold has been used here.

All the French-speaking countries in West Africa—Burkina Faso, the Ivory Coast, Senegal, and so forth—also use a regular kind of money called CFA. To get that money, of course, you have to sell things, and if you don't have something to sell, then you basically live without it. You have to stay with the old ways of bartering. The two systems of trade exist side by side.

We grow many things. For example, there are three

different kinds of millet. One of them is called sorghum in the West. We have red and white sorghum, and we have another kind of millet, which is called *ʒiè* in Dagara. We have red beans, black-eyed peas, peanuts, and we have big African yams—not the regular yams like you have here, but yams up to three feet long, weighing twenty, thirty pounds. And then we have sweet potatoes, two different kinds.

We raise animals also—chickens, guinea hens, pigs, goats, and lambs. They are raised not only for food, but also for trade. For example, if I have a goat and I need millet, we might negotiate a fair amount of grain for me to receive in return for my goat.

We hunt wild animals. But now we mainly see hunting in a context of ritual, such as initiation. It's not like in the old days when the whole tribe would take one or two months and go hunting and then come back home with meat to live on for the year.

This has changed only in the past ten years or so because of political restrictions. Basically, the government is trying to claim the land. Until the 1980s the land had always been the land of the people. Still, people did not consider it their own. They saw it as spirit, as something that they were just borrowing. Now that the government is regulating the land, you have to pay taxes on it.

During colonial times, many things changed in the Dagara people's lives. But matters such as family structure and the way people approach leadership remain much the same. Those who have gone to school in the cities are absolutely affected; they see things completely differently. But most of the villages I know of still have the ways they used to, with an almost medieval way of leadership.

There isn't one chief who is in charge of everything, who gives directions that everybody has to follow. We still have a system where elders oversee the village, without a sense of acquiring wealth and power. Power, you see, is understood in the village as very dangerous if not used correctly. So everybody is very cautious about using any kind of power over others.

Tribal people are starting to experience immense cultural pressures because of the exodus of rural youth to the cities and their exposure to mass media. Slowly but surely we are seeing, with pain, a gradual reduction of the village population and the import of all these new ideas pertaining to romance and privacy. This is what happens when young people go to the city and then come back.

In Africa, at least in the Dagara villages, buildings are mainly there for sleeping, for ritual space, and for storing food. But the actual life of the village is outside; you wouldn't have any particular place where you would go and change a diaper, for instance. It would happen right outside. You would bathe at the river and dress and groom yourself outside. You would go to the bathroom outside and use leaves from the nearby tree. Talk about cultural conflict for those who despise the old ways!

In tribal life, one is forced to slow down, to experience the now and commune with the earth and nature. Patience is a must; no one seems to understand the meaning of hurry up.

In the village we have what we refer to as elders; they are the ones who make the decisions of the village. When there is some pressing situation, the elders will get together and try to figure out what should be done. We do not have police or anything like that; we rely mainly on spirit and on the elders for justice.

Among the elders there's a council of ten that takes care of the rituals and other village concerns. They're a sort of committee within the larger group of elders. What you have to understand is that elders are not attracted to being part of this council, because it involves a lot of work. You work for the whole community, and you are not like a person in power who decides everything. People can come any time of the day to get you for help. You can be sleeping, somebody will knock on your door, and then you have to work. You don't have a choice.

This council is selected by all of those who have gone through the elder initiation. They are selected according to the Dagara understanding of the elemental forces that form the universe. We have five different elements: earth, water, mineral, fire, and nature. Each one of these elements is represented on the council by a woman and a man; the council is thus made up of five female and five male elders.

The element earth is responsible for our groundedness, our sense of identity, and our ability to nurture and to support one another.

Water is peace, focus, wisdom, and reconciliation.

Mineral helps us to remember our purpose and gives us the means to communicate and to make sense out of what others are saying.

Fire is about dreaming, keeping our connection to the self and to the ancestors, and keeping our visions alive.

Nature helps us to be our true self, to go through major changes and life-threatening situations. It brings magic and laughter.

When a member of the council of elders dies and they need, for example, a new water female, all the initiated elders gather to select a new water female for the council. Actually, you have to lobby a lot in order to find another elder, because this is not a nine-to-five job where you can let yourself be content with things and because of the delicate nature of the job.

The family in Africa is always extended. You would never refer to your cousin as "cousin," because that would be an insult. So your cousins are your sisters and brothers. Your nieces are your children. Your uncles are your fathers. Your aunts are your mothers. Your sister's husband is your husband, and your brother's wife is your wife.

Children are also encouraged to call other people outside the family mothers and fathers, sisters and brothers.

In the village, extended families live in the same compound. The women sleep on one side of the house, the men on the other.

The children are allowed to sleep wherever they feel like. They are not restricted until they reach adolescence. They can sleep with the women today, move to the men's quarters tomorrow, or sleep with their grandfather or grandmother, and so on.

This concept of the big family is really helpful. I remember when I was a kid, I had the choice of a different father every day, depending on my mood. So if I wanted one of my uncles to be my father for the day, I would focus all my attention on that person and ignore the others. And the others wouldn't take it personally, because they saw it as an opportunity for me to decide what I wanted. This also allows a large number of people in the village to acknowledge the child and to see her or his spirit.

CHAPTER 2

A SONG OF SPIRIT

Intimacy in general terms is a song of spirit inviting two people to come and share their spirit together. It is a song that no one can resist. We hear it while awake or sleeping, in community or alone. We cannot ignore it.

There is a spiritual dimension to every relationship, no matter what its origins, whether it is acknowledged as spiritual or not. Two people come together because spirit wants them together. What is important now is to look at the relationship as spirit-driven, instead of driven by the individual.

The role of spirit in our relationships is to be the driver, to monitor our relationships for the good. Its purpose is to help us to be better people, to bind us in such a way that we maintain our connection, not only with ourselves, but also with the great beyond. Spirit helps us fulfill our own life purpose and maintain our sanity.

When indigenous people talk about spirit, they are basically referring to the life force in everything. For instance, you might refer to the spirit in an animal, that is, the life force in that animal, which can help us accomplish our life purpose and maintain our connection to the spirit world.

The spirit of the human being is the same way. In our tradition, each of us is seen as a spirit who has taken the form of a human in order to carry out a purpose. Spirit is the energy that helps us connect, that helps us see beyond our racially limited parameters, and also helps us in ritual and in connecting with the ancestors.

Ancestors are also referred to as spirits. The spirit of an ancestor has the capacity to see not only into the invisible spirit world but also into this world, and it serves as our eyes on both sides. It is this power of ancestors that will help us direct our lives and avoid falling into huge ditches.

Ancestor spirits can see future, past, and present. They can see inside of us and outside of us. They can see cross-dimensionally. And they're lucky not to have physical bodies as we do, because without the limitation of the body, they have the fluidity of an eye that sees many different ways, many different directions.

There are many different spirits in Africa, and each of them has a particular role to play, or something they can assist us with. There is the spirit of the earth, which is responsible for our identity, our comfort, our nourishment, and so on. And there's the spirit of nature, the spirit of the river, the spirit of the mountain. There is the spirit of the animals, of the water, the spirit of the ancestors. Spirit is everywhere.

This world of spirit involves and affects absolutely everyone in the world. Without spirit, we would have never made it here. Without spirit, it would be really hard to know whether we were going to wake up tomorrow and be alive. It would be really hard to know we have life.

People in the West can begin to strengthen their intimate relationships by maintaining their connection with spirit—

through prayers, through walking in nature and dealing with natural forces, through connecting with the earth, the mineral, the fire, or the mountains. By spending time in nature and taking time away from the mundane day-to-day way of living, we allow the part of ourselves that can hear natural beings to listen, so that we can find our connection to those spirits.

It is very easy for us to get lost in the mundane world and forget about our connection to spirit. Yet without that connection we are basically the walking dead.

We can also strengthen our connection to spirit through ritual. Various rituals help us to heal particular wounds and open us to spirit's call.

When we talk about connecting with the spirits of ancestors, many people assume that we refer to our own direct ancestors. But this is difficult. Many of us don't even know our grandfathers. There is such a thing as the pool of ancestors—it doesn't have to be a person or spirit we know or can imagine. It can be the tree out there. It can be the cows out there, your dog or cat at home. Your great-great-grandfather who died many generations ago may have joined a great ensemble of spirits to the point where you can't even identify him. He's probably the creek running down over there.

So what is important is to realize that any person who has lost the physical body is a potential ancestor. And by simply expressing your longing for the support of ancestors, you will attract a lot of spirits.

When you start a ritual where you need their support, if you address them simply as spirits or ancestors, maybe even say, "the ones who I know, and the ones who I don't know, and those who know me more than I do myself," you are tapping the ancestral power out there, and you are not beginning with confusion as to whether, in the pool of ancestors, there is a spirit out there that you can identify with.

We might think that the confusion we experience in our daily life happens in isolation, but in reality it has something to do with our lack of connection to our ancestors. The idea of healing our ancestors can be helpful in this context. For the Dagara people, grief is a way for us to bridge the gap between ourselves and our ancestors. A grieving ritual can release the anger and sadness over a dead relative and carry his spirit to the land of the ancestors, where it can be of use to us. And through a regular feeding of our ancestors we can renew our ties with them.

In a relationship there is a natural tendency for the spirits within two people to come together. When two spirits can commune and really share at the deepest level without having the mind interfere, the two people are bonded in a very strong, sincere, and loving way.

When spirit is taken away, then we let our ego take care of relationship problems or simply overshadow them in order for us to feel good. As a result, we may think that we are in control of ourselves and our relationships, but in fact we are not—as we are bound to find out, when things start to fall apart.

Once an intimate relationship is taken out of its spiritual context, it faces many dangers. A deep disconnection is created, not only on the spiritual plane, but also at the personal level.

People involved in a solely sexual relationship, for instance, carry within themselves a huge energetic hole from early childhood wounds that completely cuts them off from their true selves. Their hope is that the person with whom they are involved might give them the connection they crave. More often than not, the person they are reaching out to does not have a connection to the self either. And so you have two people who are disconnected at both the spiritual and the personal level. The relationship doesn't have any kind of grounding force or foundation to hold it.

Children in the cities of West Africa are already cut off from the day-to-day life connected to spirit. This is because they live apart from the village. When they go to school, they don't learn about spirit or work on their connection to it. They don't learn about their traditions. They go to schools in order to learn things that aren't spirit-based and to forget about their traditional ways.

The first Dagara people who went to study in the cities and felt the influence of the French colonizers came back feeling ashamed about their own parents and the traditional way of life. Some of them remained in the cities and have spent twenty years there without again setting foot in the village. The only time these people turn back to spirit is when their life is on the line. If they're having problems with their job, if somebody is threatening to kill them, if they want to stay in power, if they are sick, then they will seek help from the elders and from the healers. But until then, they're completely disconnected from spirit.

And so, you have to always understand the mind of these people who have been to school. There are few who come out of it still connected with spirit.

I see so many romantic relationships in the West being driven by control and ego. To bring these relationships back to health, people must begin to see that spirit is behind their being together and to put control and ego aside.

If you are reading this book, I would say that at least you have not completely erased spirit from your existence. It means that there is an ear that is still listening. The spirit is still at work. And for those people who still have this channel to spirit open within them, it is like a magnetic force that pulls them.

The first thing to do now is to say, "I've heard you, spirit. I may not know what to do, but I know that I just heard you." And from then on, start to release the control and the ego that ride in your relationships; bring spirit from the background, from the dark corner where it has been a useless thing.

If the parties involved in a relationship can begin to open themselves up to spirit in this way, what the relationship is supposed to be will evolve. Whether it's a love relationship, a family relationship, or friendship, it will flow from the recognition that spirit, not ego and control, is the first driver.

This is not the kind of book that tells you, if you had a fight with your husband, to go to page 100 or 300 and all shall be fixed thereafter. It's too easy for people to fall prey again to control when they're being spoon-fed with step one, do this, step two, do that. It's very easy to go back to that control place again, instead of recognizing that our relationships are spirit-based. What we need to say is "Okay, spirit, I finally heard you. Now, what is the next step?"

Separation from spirit, as we see here in the West, causes a greater emphasis on romantic love. It creates a vortex of longing for another person, for another way of connecting. Yet romantic love is only a way of finding that other connection, which is to spirit, that we are actually looking for.

The coming together of two spirits gives birth to a new spirit. You can call it the spirit of the relationship or the spirit of intimacy. It is very important because it acts as a barometer of the relationship, and it must be nurtured and kept alive. If that spirit dies, then the relationship dies.

Rituals are done in the village with respect to that spirit. There is a ritual done once a year in order to amend whatever has happened to this spirit, to bring it back to life if there has been disconnection. I like to call this ritual the bringing of two souls together. People in the West may not like this, but it is done through sacrifice.

We must try not to educate our children away from the spirit, so that they don't have to work so hard trying to reconnect when they grow up. When they know they already have spirit, then everything else becomes understood. And it makes life easier for them.

This is how to succeed as a parent: acknowledge that there is a powerful spirit present that should be honored instead of taken away. This is also how to succeed in a relationship.

CHAPTER 3

THE EMBRACE OF COMMUNITY

Community is the spirit, the guiding light of the tribe, whereby people come together in order to fulfill a specific purpose, to help others fulfill their purpose, and to take care of one another. The goal of the community is to make sure that each member of the community is heard and is properly giving the gifts he has brought to this world. Without this giving, the community dies. And without the community, the individual is left without a place where he can contribute. The community is that grounding place where people come and share their gifts and receive from others.

When you don't have community, you are not listened to; you don't have a place you can go to and feel that you really belong. You don't have people to affirm who you are and to support you in bringing forward your gifts. This disempowers the psyche, making you vulnerable to consumerism and all the things that come along with it.

Also, it leaves many people who have wonderful contributions to make holding back their gifts, not knowing where to put them. And without the unloading of our gifts we experience a blockage inside, which affects us spiritually, mentally, and physically in many different ways. We are left without a home to go to when we need to be seen.

One of the principles of the Dagara concept of a relationship is that it's not private. When we talk about "our relationship" in the village, the word *our* is not limited to two. And this is why we find it pretty hard to live a relationship in a modern culture that is lacking true community. In the absence of community, two people are forced to say, "This relationship is ours," when in fact, a community should be claiming ownership.

The absence of a true community leaves a couple totally responsible for themselves and anything else around them. It narrows down their ways of getting needs met, so that their relationship becomes their community. And if it is not able to fulfill this role, then the individuals begin to feel like a failure. It affects the psyche so dramatically that they feel that there's no place for them. What they thought was their support group, their partnership, is unable to satisfy their needs.

It's very strange to regard two people as a community. Where is everybody else? On my first visit home after moving to the United States, I told my mother just Malidoma and I lived in this house. She thought I was the craziest person she'd seen; to her, living like this is inconceivable. It means that there isn't any kind of outside energy coming to give support and strength to our relationship, and that we are basically left on our own to figure things out, which is absolutely impossible.

You know, with one person, it's hard to see very far. Two people, you can see a little more. But if you have a whole group of people around really caring about you and telling you, "You are doing the right thing! We want you to be around! Give us your gifts!" it helps you fulfill your purpose. Even the most stubborn people will get beyond their stubbornness in order to work on their life purpose. But with just two people, it's really too much to ask. Or even with the nuclear family.

In my own marriage I bring as many people as I can into the relationship. We also get back home as much as possible. How do we bring more people in? We constantly monitor the relationship and, through ritual, create community to give us the support we need. This fuels us so that we can continue what we are doing here.

When there are collisions in my marriage, I call upon this community. I know that without their help, the fire of our relationship might have been extinguished.

Here in the West we may never have the kind of community we had back in Africa, but at least we can have a sense of it by allowing friends to be a part of what we are doing. Fifteen minutes of communication with others can help in a deep way to make up for a lack of community.

Friends and family provide you with a container, a safe container, where you can go if you need support—if you need help with ritual, if you need somebody to give you a hug, if you need to talk to somebody and get another perspective on something.

You are free to do whatever you want with the advice they give you, but it helps to bring the spirits of other people into your life; it gives you many more eyes to see and helps overcome limitations. Sometimes you will be spiritually blind to something, and a friend can be aware of that very thing. If you don't reach out to friends and family, your reality can become pretty limited; with the input of these people, it widens.

Friends and family can also take away from intimate relationships. The blessing of the family is very important when it comes to intimacy, but if there are unresolved issues in one's family, it can affect the life of a person, even in an intimate space with somebody else.

When couples don't get the blessing of the community, most of the time it will create a vacuum that you have to work hard to compensate for or heal. Many people have divorced simply because of the pressure from the community, family, or friends who did not support the marriage or even have a spiritual understanding of the relationship.

It's hard for a relationship to survive without that support. Some couples stay together, but it takes a toll. Take, for instance, somebody who is in a relationship and needs friends or family to do a ritual for her, or to simply hear her, but doesn't have access to them. Who can she turn to? Therapy is good, but it can only take you so far. It's really hard for therapists to compensate for everything.

When you don't have a community of friends and family involved in a relationship, it makes you base all your intimate expectations on your marriage. And that is really hard; that is too much to ask of any one relationship. Of course, your partner is your friend and family, but to receive everything from that person is absolutely impossible.

When people get their friends and family involved, they can make intimacy work. But people, you know, they think things are private, and that they have to keep everything to themselves. Keeping everything private usually kills a relationship.

Most of the time our crises are not complicated. When we keep them private they grow fatter every day, and then they start to strangle us. So we must be open to other people in order for our relationships to work. I notice that many people who are in women's groups, for instance, or men's groups are able to put aside the fear of talking with others about their problems, and I think this is good. Problems in relationships will always be with us, but to let fear of sharing threaten your future is ridiculous.

People in the West can create a sense of community in their cities just as people in West Africa have. They can do this by providing one another with continuous support. Each of us needs something to hang on to. That's why you have all these small communities here and there—a group of women working on social issues, a group of men, and all these small groups pursuing a common goal. They are attempts to re-create a piece of that greater community that used to be and that has been destroyed.

The only difference is that most of these communities don't focus on spirit. They tend to leave spirit outside of their activity, which is a mistake. It's another way of saying. "We are in control," when in fact a true community must be based on spirit. Spirit should be the leader and the guide for everybody in a community.

One can argue that churches constitute such a community in the West. That would be the case if there were a way for churches to empower individuals. Then we would begin to approach the kind of community we are talking about with the village. But people do not go to church to reaffirm that spirit is inside them and that everyone is directly connected to spirit. You won't find a church where everyone gives out the Eucharist to one another.

It may be hard for people who have lived all their life in the West to regard everything they own as belonging to the whole community, but this is the case in the village. As a result, each person in the village contributes to the well-being of others.

When you have a child, for instance, it's not just your child, it's the child of the community. From birth onward, the mother is not the only one who is responsible for a child. Anybody else can feed and nurture the child. If another woman has a baby, she can breast-feed any child. And it's perfectly all right.

Sometimes, when a mother wants to see her child, she can't because so many people are caring for him. I remember I used to trick my sisters all the time. I would go and get their children and disappear with them for a long time. My sisters would be wondering where the kids were, but they knew they were in safe hands.

When you get married in this kind of context, it's not only you who gets married, it's the whole tribe. Every single person in that tribe, in that village, in your family, is going to get married that day. You are the one giving them the opportunity to do that. And so people in the village will say, "I'm getting married on such and such day," even though it is someone else's actual wedding.

If a child grows up with the idea that Mom and Dad are her or his only community, then when she has a problem, if the parents cannot fix it, she doesn't have anybody else to turn to. The parents alone are responsible for whoever the child becomes, and this is a little bit too much to ask of just two people. And many times, only one person is left to serve as parent.

Giving a child a broader sense of community helps her not to rely on one person. Then the child can go to a person of her choice, and if that person cannot fix her problem, she can go to somebody else.

Because we are human beings, we are restricted as to what we can do or give. So in raising children we definitely need the support of other people. It's like we say in the village: "It takes a whole village to raise a child." It's also true to say, "It takes a whole village to keep parents sane."

When couples have children without a community to support them, they don't have much time to work out whatever is going on between themselves. And so things pile up, and when their children are gone, they suddenly realize that there is this mountain of things that has not been dealt with for years. And so they start to dig in, and when they cannot resolve their problems—you know what people do. They leave without even saying good-bye. A lot of people divorce after their children leave home; I think the absence of community support in child-rearing is one of the main causes.

How can we move toward a more sane family structure or relationship structure? The main thing I see at this point is community—building communities where you can trust one another, where you can help a mother who is crying because she has a child who is crying and she doesn't know what to give to her.

You know, in the village, when you get up in the morning, the first thing you do is to go outside. But here, one day I was sitting all day inside without going out, and it occurred to me that this was the first time in my life I'd ever done that, except when I wasn't feeling well.

To get up in the morning and not go out among people is absolutely inconceivable to somebody in the village. Because when you stay all day inside, it means that something isn't going right with you, and people worry about you. And so we can begin by going outside, talking to our neighbors and helping each other out.

It's small steps like this. It's like what we say: If you have a baby, you don't throw her away because she's small. You keep her and keep nurturing her, knowing that one day she's going to be a grown-up. So these are the kinds of smart things we can do, nurturing many small relationships so that one day community can happen.

In the village, people cannot believe that just Malidoma and I live in a whole house. It's completely inconceivable. They wonder why we have a whole house, especially when I tell them that it is really big compared with the houses we have in the village. "It's really huge!" I told my mother, and she just shook her head and said, "What are you doing this for?" I explained to her that everybody has his own place and there's no village to go to. There's no family where we live. I told her, "You might want to come and live with me." And she said, "No. Not under those conditions."

It is as difficult for indigenous people to conceive of life without a community as it is for most Westerners to imagine life in a community.

To create a community that will work for people here, there is a need to look carefully at some of the fundamentals of a healthy community—spirit, children, elders, responsibility, gift-giving, accountability, ancestors, and ritual. These elements form the base of a community. And it doesn't have to start with a lot of people. I'd rather have a circle of a few good friends and be a community with them than just get lost in a crowd of people who don't care at all.

Intimacy, the natural attraction of two human beings to each other, is something that the elders say is actually prompted by spirit, and spirit brings people together in order to give them the opportunity to grow together. That growth is directly connected to the gifts that two people are capable of providing to the village. And this is why when a couple is in trouble, the whole village is in trouble.

People in the village will involve themselves in the problems of a couple and dissect them and make sure that they fix them because their interests are at risk. So community support is not entirely altruistic. People are not necessarily coming to help the couple. They are coming to help themselves. If a couple is in trouble, those around them may not get what they need.

When we start to feel a problem, we tend to think it's just two people who are involved and we forget about the fact that spirit is there. We tend to forget that we have allies who can bring us strength. We forget to ask for help from friends or family members.

In the village, it's easier for people because every morning when you wake up somebody will come and ask you, "Did you hear something sweet last night?" And if you remain silent or you say no, then the person will get worried because something is wrong. If you didn't hear something good, it means that something sour must have taken the place of the good. They will then get to the bottom of that problem before it gets out of control.

It's not surprising every morning to see women just gather and start to talk about things and, if need be, go toward the bushes and start to walk away from the compound because there is something that needs to be taken care of. This reminds me of the importance that gender plays in relationships. Without help from people of the same gender it's pretty hard to maintain a balance in your relationship. A woman should not expect her husband to take the place of her women friends and to care for her in the same way. Similarly, a man should not expect his wife to take the place of male friends.

Being a woman does not mean you have nothing to do with masculine energy. Similarly, being a man does not mean you have nothing to do with the feminine. Vaginas and penises are not the only things that define our sexual nature. Our lives are influenced by the presence within us of both feminine and masculine energies. It is important that these energies maintain harmony within us.

There are things that men do in order to nourish what they call their female self and things that women have to do in order to nourish their male self. In the village, once

35

a year, men who have gone through initiation together meet at the same spot where they were initiated and have a ritual that looks something like mothering. Their behavior is a kind of strict male-to-male emotional exchange. There's something about it that breaks down the narcissistic feeling that comes with managing responsibilities.

Even though it's not a funeral (where men, women, and children can cry together), the men cry as much as they want. There's a need to reawaken the part of the self that is in touch with emotion, and this ritual allows them to do so without waiting until somebody dies.

There is a caretaking, not prescribed, but a random caretaking, that goes on. Someone, because of inner pressure of some sort, will break down, and someone else will take care of him. And while taking care of him, the caretaker too is going to break down, and someone is going to come and join them. So it becomes a continuous support and nurturing ritual.

It makes it easier for some reason, when the men come back, for them to stop feeling that they have to invoke some kind of control within the ritual space of intimacy. In other words, when the sense of responsibility and of being a man in the community stops overwhelming someone who has participated in this ritual, the circle of intimacy they create with their partner becomes closer to what spirit wants.

The belief is that the male tends to put on his warrior mode even in the ash circle of intimacy. When that warrior self has not been tamed by some kind of motherly energy, it is almost impossible for a man to engage in intimate relations with his partner.

In the village, in order for the feminine and the masculine energies to live harmoniously, women and men must commit themselves to work at balancing their sexual energies. When either energy dominates, it becomes overpowering and can threaten the stability of the village. For this reason women not only gather up on a yearly basis with their initiation sisters, but they also get together as often as they can and go to a cave or go to the bush. There we do a set of rituals in order to build our masculine energy by acting out our rage and anger and by taking on men's roles.

Then we go hunting, even though killing is not the emphasis of the ritual because women usually do not kill in the village. It allows women to be outwardly. This is usually followed by the warriors' dance that young men learn while being initiated into manhood. All women dress like men throughout the duration of the ritual. Some women wear beards and mustaches.

Usually the *purè*, the "female father," is there, and she will ensure that the masculine energy is being built. If you did not know her beforehand, you would think that she was a man. The tone of her voice, the look of her eyes, and everything else about her carries masculine energy. One by one, the women go to her. First there is a foot-to-foot connection, then a head-to-head connection. This helps to seal the experience.

When we go back home there is a small welcoming ritual. We are all received into our homes in such a way that we don't start to build upon our renewed masculine energy and become completely masculine, nor do we go back to being completely in the feminine energy.

We accept the tradition that women must work with women in order to build a feminine identity and that men must work with men in order to build a masculine identity. This way, when a man and a woman come together, they are better able to relate to each other.

There is something in the indigenous world that compels gender groups to get together in order to work certain things out. I see similar practices in the West in what is called feminism and in the men's movement. These are ways for women and men to better their relationships, not only with their gender, but also with the other sex.

You will notice in many villages in Africa that during the days women are all together, men are all together also. This is not a sexist practice. It's just that for some reason there's a feeling that a clear sense of otherness is essential to a harmonious coming together with your mate.

Today we are not called upon to wage war with the opposite gender. We need to embrace the new millennium with a brand-new eye, a new heart, one that allows for mutual respect. Women and men live their own mysteries, and neither gender will ever fully grasp the other. The model of the village is there not to encourage sexism, nor to make men and women the same, but to create an environment in which both genders appreciate and honor the other.

CHAPTER 4

RITUAL: THE CALL TO SPIRIT

It's important in any relationship to do ritual—in order to keep peace, to ground ourselves, and to create better communication. There are rituals that help couples to reaffirm their purpose, to give their gifts to the community, and to address difficulties in the lives of others so that they are not just wrapped up in their own things.

What is a ritual? A ritual is a ceremony in which we call in spirit to come and be the driver, the overseer of our activities. The elements of ritual allow us to connect with the self, the community, and the natural forces around us. In ritual we call in spirit to show us obstacles that we cannot see because of our limitations as human beings. Rituals help us to remove blocks standing between us and our true spirit and other spirits.

In the village, everybody is addicted to ritual. There people experience intimacy not just with their partners but with the rest of the village, at all times, simply because of the repeated involvement with ritual. There's such a high from this that most conversations are about the ritual that just ended, or about the need for the next one. Maybe that's why they don't have television.

They need to be constantly involved in ritual because it's like an energy that gives a high that lasts, perhaps three or four days, and as soon as they start coming down, everybody is concerned. They need the high again.

You don't do a ritual just for the sake of doing a ritual. Every ritual must have a very specific purpose, a clearly stated intention. It must have something to resolve.

There are personal rituals, community rituals, maintenance rituals, and radical rituals. Radical rituals are done to disassociate someone from a state of profound turmoil or alienation and reunite him with his spirit. They are done by a community for an individual or individuals. It is then necessary to do regular maintenance rituals in order for the effects of the ritual to continue.

Take, for instance, a person who is very disconnected from himself, from his spirit. He doesn't need a maintenance ritual. He needs something radical to end that disconnection and bring the spirit back into himself so that he can start to be alive again.

In such a ritual, the community must be there because a person becomes so vulnerable that he needs a contained sacred space held by other people who will make sure that he doesn't hurt himself. And also the community must be there to welcome him back. Even though a person experiences a radical ritual, if he doesn't have an appropriate welcoming back, his psyche will take it as meaning that he did not do it right. He may have to go back and do it again. The psyche won't know the ritual has been successful without a community there to acknowledge that this is so.

Every time you want to move into a ritual, you need to recognize that there's a whole line of ancestors behind you, there's a whole spirit world around you, there is the animal world, the ground world, the trees, and so forth. If you have a way of saying to these forces, "Come and be with us in such a way that we can feel and do such-and-such," then you're already in ritual.

Next, you must state your purpose, being quite specific about your need or goals. Spirits are drawn to a place of activity, particularly activity that interests them and demands their involvement.

All you need to do from then on is to go deep into your heart and listen to the rhythm of it. There is a language spoken to you by the beings you have called into your circle. The problem is, we usually don't listen enough, and therefore we don't hear it.

Usually, if you ask one spirit to come, it will not come alone. It gathers its friends, its relatives, friends of its friends, and so on. And all these spirits will come to you. You don't need a Ph.D. or to suffer pain and contortions in order to attract them. All you really need is the sincerity of your heart and a willing ear.

In the West, people tend to standardize everything. So if you describe one ritual, people think it applies to all situations. Even though every case is different, people will follow the same formula. In ritual, that doesn't work. A ritual has to be made specific to the people who are involved in it. And if you try to standardize things, you actually take away the spirit of the people and try to force something false into the situation.

We think that someone must bring a secret book of ritual recipes so that if we have a toothache, we go to page 129, read paragraph 2, and that will take care of it. When in fact we ourselves *are* page 129, paragraph 2! So I'm saying, trust in yourself, believe in your ability to hear. Just say, "I know these things exist somewhere in me."

I remember growing up, how one of my grandmothers used to involve us in ritual. She would create situations where we would have to come up with an appropriate ritual. She would never interfere with our creativity. All she would do was make sure that we were making progress. Just like a mother with a baby learning to walk, she would guide us a little, and when we fell she would give us encouragement and strength to keep on trying.

With any ritual, you start by preparing the sacred space and constructing a shrine; then call in spirit with an invocation. It has to start with the setting of the intention, and with a group of committed people who want the greatest good to happen.

The people involved in a ritual are the only ones who can determine exactly what elements are needed. Rituals are not alike, they each have their own flavor. It would be best to look at each situation with care, then determine the elements that are needed. The fun comes when everybody adds an ingredient here and there.

In this way, a ritual is like a meal where everybody brings an ingredient. Some people bring onions, some people bring tomatoes, some people bring lettuce or celery or pepper or chili, and so on. After gathering all the elements, then you look and see which ingredients work best.

A ritual begins when you define a ritual space. You can delineate a ritual space with ash, leaves, or stones, or sometimes just by building a shrine.

Select a place where you can build a shrine and light candles. Take ash, and make a circle as big as you think it needs to be. It could be a small circle for two people to sit in and communicate for conflict resolution or a big space to include many people. The ash can be from any burnt wood, preferably free of nails or any kind of chemical. Because ash is connected to fire, it provides protection. It helps when calling in the spirits and helps people connect. It prevents negative energies from creeping in while you're in ritual.

Your shrine should be made of items that symbolize something good for you and relate to the purpose of the ritual. It should be made beautiful. You could use such things as candles, water, flowers, textiles, masks, or pictures. In a ritual done for a relationship, it is sometimes useful to set up a couple shrine and a personal shrine. A couple shrine will have elements contributed by both people, and the personal shrine will be designed by the individual.

In the Dagara tribe, we would use colors such as blue-black, red, yellow, green, and white for the shrine. These colors represent, respectively, water, fire, earth, nature, and mineral. (Dagara people don't distinguish between blue and black.) We would use rocks to represent the mineral kingdom, leaves for the nature kingdom. The skull in a relationship ritual represents death and memory; green leaves represent life. We would bring in water to represent peace, the state of peace we would like to have in our life. Soil would symbolize nurturing, groundedness, a sense of identity and support. Fire would be represented by ash, blood, something red to symbolize our connection to the ancestors. Bones and rocks mean communication and our ability to remember. Depending on our needs, one or more of these elements would be used in a ritual.

So, if it's a ritual for peace, for example, you can use blue or black candles, some water, and other items that say "peace" to you.

If the ritual is for nurturing or groundedness or working on the identity of a relationship, you would use yellow candles and soil.

If you're working on communication, on making sure that you interpret correctly the signs you receive from your partner, you'd choose a white candle, rocks, and bones.

If you are working on connecting with the spirit of the ancestors or keeping the spiritual connection in your relationship, you would use red candles. Fire, you know, brings warmth, action, and compassion. It helps a couple to dream together. But I tell people to be sure that their intention is set absolutely right and clear for the use of red, because the velocity of fire can quickly degenerate into war.

Then, if you're looking for magic to help you go through major changes, or, let's say, a couple is starting to put on masks before the community, acting insincerely and presenting their false side, green candles and fabrics are used, along with masks—which represent the great mystery—and anything else that reminds one of nature.

These elements of ritual are to be taken simply as a source of inspiration, particularly for those who do not have a background in ritual.

Now that you have your space delineated, your shrine ready, and the purpose of the ritual determined and clearly expressed to the spirits and ancestors, you can help the person for whom the ritual is designed. You might say that now the ritual starts, but in fact, the ritual started when people first gathered to figure things out and began, with the guidance of spirit, to prepare the ritual space.

We should never exclude children from ritual. When children are present, the most simple and vibrant rituals become possible. If they are there, whatever you do wrong is right. For some reason they are, by their own nature, naturally ritualistic. Even if it means just to get them together, call on the spirits, state your purpose, and have a procession where they lead and you follow, that's all right. Because the amount of sincerity and purity that is in front of you will heal all kinds of dirt or criticism or negativity that you may carry. It's that powerful.

Not everything in ritual from Africa can work here, like the idea of sacrifice—sacrificing a chicken, for instance. But people here are familiar with offerings. Take an offering to the sea. Take an offering to the mountain or to a field. It is very helpful, periodically, to give something away on behalf of your intimate life—an offering of gratitude to spirit, or a giveaway of negativity to cleanse your relationship.

People have a tendency to stay away from emotion, so we disconnect ourselves from what is happening and it becomes superficial. In ritual, if tears are coming, it's okay for tears to be there. If anger is coming, it's important that anger come out. In fact, anger carries in it a healing energy. Only when we let it overtake our being and keep it prisoner does it becomes destructive.

The whole concept of the intimate is primarily derived from ritual. Outside of ritual, nothing can be truly intimate. Which is why, in the village, every emotion is ritualistically understood. So human relationships, when they begin to deepen, enter into the canal of ritual. One's closest relationships are constantly happening as ritual.

So, anything close, anything intimate, is impossible without a ritual space. Anything that brings people to express to one another something other than normal day-to-day life touches on the spiritual world, on the ancestral world, and therefore is a ritual event.

To learn how to become familiar with the intimate is to go to the school of ritual again. Because if you know how to dwell in ritual, you are likely to handle your relationship better than a person who doesn't know how. I don't know how to prove that, but I can't help but see in the screaming and yelling of a couple's conflict-resolution ritual the renewal of a contract of intimacy. It is as if somehow, without this ritual, another five days of relationship are not possible. It also means that here there are people who are not taking their relationship for granted.

If people understood the connection between intimacy and spirit, there would be a different approach to how they deal with the whole idea of relationships. And they would begin to understand that ritual can help heal the anger and frustration that can arise between partners.

In a ritual space, spirit helps to take care of those issues. It's not a quick fix—one ritual and everything is going to be perfect. Conflicts are usually deeply rooted in the psyche, and it's really hard for people to separate themselves from them. But when one starts to leave the control to spirit and to invite spirit through ritual, it's very easy for spirit to help heal those wounds.

Most of the relationships that I observe in this culture begin somewhere at the top of the hill. The top of the hill has this nice feeling of being in love. There is all this difficulty about dating, oh, it's so frustrating, you have to go out, you're scared that it won't work out, that something will collapse. But eventually everything works and it looks like paradise. This is a relationship at the top of the hill.

Now, since a relationship must grow and must be constantly in motion and it's already at the top, where is it going to go? It is very hard to figure out a way to continue circling around the top, so more often than not, it's going to go down.

In a context in which the community supports the relationship between two people, that relationship starts at the bottom of the hill. It is pushed by the community and by spirit, with the support of ritual, gradually toward the top, so that when the two people arrive at the top, they arrive there with an entire community.

What is the fate of a relationship in the absence of community? And in the absence of ritual? I think it is a pretty endangered entity. This is why those of us who are in an intimate relationship must begin to approach it as something sacred that must be dealt with in a ritual context.

How would that happen? I think the ability of two people to discover each other must first be honored with a ritual thanksgiving to spirit. Because it is through spirit that two people manage to meet. And so these two people must find a way to ritualize their encounter and give thanks to the very spirit that has brought them together. This is something that their imagination and the love that they have for each other can help them do.

The next thing is to continually return the relationship itself to the very giver of that relationship. The couple is the container, but the spirit is the one whose blessing hand injects life and growth into their relationship. Whenever conflict arises, that conflict must be seen primarily as a warning sent by spirit of a deep instability or a deviation from the path, the path drawn by spirit for the relationship. So again, it is to spirit that the people in conflict must go, through ritual, in order to realize that the conflict is something bigger than both of them put together. Maybe by humbly giving that problem into the hands of spirit, lightly may be shed on how to begin resolving it.

Emotion is very hard to resolve intellectually. That's because the mind doesn't know how to feel; its logic cannot fulfill the heart's desire. And this is why it's so important to realize how ritual, the feeling within ritual, can be a helpful tool in resolving crises that arise in a relationship. What I am trying to say here is that in a lot of ways, it's a gift from spirit that we are able to notice each other, to care for each other. But that gift cannot be taken for granted. Every gift must be maintained and nurtured. Even if we don't know how to nurture that gift, at least we must notify the giving source of our inability to take care of the gift.

Spirits love to intervene in our affairs. But they don't do it against our will. They are waiting over there for us to give them a job to do. We always talk about high unemployment in this world; just think about the other world! And so these are little odd jobs that we can throw here and there to the waiting spirits, things for them to do for us. Maybe it is through doing these little things that we will travel our blind way back to the kind of community that will naturally hold us together.

We cannot begin by figuring out in our brains exactly how a ritual will work before we get into it. We have to start by telling spirit that we recognize we don't know. There's nothing wrong in not knowing. There's something wrong in not saying you don't know. Actually spirits love to hear that you don't know because they do. And they will take it as an invitation to do what they have to do.

And so, I think that the best way, or the way still left for us, to care for our relationships is by reaching out to spirit through ritual. I think that most of you know what I mean by that. Every time you speak from the heart, invoking or telling a being from the other world that something is going on in this world, you are in ritual. You are doing something here that includes others who don't have flesh and bones like you do.

We are the eyes of the ancestors in this world. When we notice that something is not right in our relationships, it is our responsibility to notify the ancestors. But if we keep seeing things that are not right and we continue to struggle with them—perhaps because we think we are not creative enough or do not deserve to be helped or do not know how to ask for help—then we run the risk of wasting our time on things that are the business of our allies in the other world. In the meantime, our real purpose is left waiting.

CHAPTER 5

BORN TO A PURPOSE

When two people are married and have built an intimate relationship, there is a desire that they make themselves available for other souls to come through, that they create a safe and sacred space for spirits who want to bring their gifts and fulfill their purpose.

And so people in our village would say that children do not belong completely to the parents who gave them birth. They have used their parents' bodies to come through, but they belong to the community and to the spirit.

Each person chooses her or his life purpose before he or she is even born. I, for example, chose to work with the great mysteries, to explore the unknown, to let myself be swallowed by the mysteries so that others might learn. And I made the commitment to travel outside of the village someday so that others might see into the unknown and remember the old rituals.

Now, how is one's purpose learned? When a woman is pregnant, a hearing ritual is performed. In this ritual, elders will ask the unborn child, "Who are you? Why are you coming here? Why do you bother, this world is too messed up. What can we do to ease your journey?"

The baby takes over the mother's voice and speaks back, "This is who I am. I am coming to help uphold the knowledge of the ancestors," or, "I am coming to do this and this." And based on that information, the elders will prepare an appropriate ritual space in which to receive the child and make sure that everything is ready here before the child is born.

After the birth, the elders make sure they surround the child with things that will help her remember and accomplish the purpose she has described. And when she reaches adolescence and goes through initiation, she has to go back to the time before she was born to remember what she said. This is because growing up is a process of forgetting; this body, as the elders say, takes away certain things from us as we grow. Up until the age of five or six, children remember things perfectly, but after that something starts to happen in the body that makes them forget.

At the hearing ritual the baby might choose a stone and gives a description of what the stone will look like. The elders will go out and locate the stone by the way it moves or behaves. And that stone, basically, contains all the information about the person. It is through this stone, sitting back in the medicine room in my village, that the elders can monitor what's happening with me here right now.

When we come together with another person, we create a foundation that allows us to fulfill the life purpose with which we were born. Our partner, if chosen well, will have been born to a purpose along the same path. If our purpose and that of our partner are in conflict, then it is felt at a personal and communal level. We feel it in our intimate lives. Take, for instance, a peacemaker and someone who is the source of a nuclear war. Their life purposes take them on two completely separate roads. They do not have anything in common. They have no ground to uphold their intimate connection.

Each of us is born into one of the five Dagara elemental groups. This element shapes our purpose in life and can play a role in the selection of a partner. One's element is determined by one's birth year: there are nature years, water years, fire years, mineral years, and earth years. People choose, before birth, to come in a certain year in order to fulfill their life purpose. My element is nature.

If your birth year ends in a 0 or 5—that is, you might be born in 1950 or 1965—you are an earth person; if it ends in 1 or 6, you are a water baby; 2 and 7 are fire; 3 and 8 are nature; 4 and 9 are mineral. Even though you start from one given element, you have to contain all five in order to be able to function. And when you are lacking in one element, it can show.

These numbers might seem arbitrary to many people in the West, but they were not determined randomly. They have their roots in a deep understanding of the universe. Each number carries an energy, which affects us regardless of our background.

I always like to go as far back as birth and the manner in which a person was welcomed as a newborn in order to see if that influences the kind of relationship that person ends up having. Birth is the arrival of somebody from another place; the person who is arriving must be welcomed, must be made to feel that she has arrived in a place where there are human beings who will receive her gifts.

The absence of a welcoming village around a newborn may inadvertently erase something in the psyche; that loss, later on in life, will be felt like a huge gap. Although this person will feel a strong need to connect with others, he may have difficulty reaching out for support from a community he fears might reject him. What would this person be seeking when he enters into an intimate relationship if not to bridge that gap?

But a problem arises when he realizes that his partner alone cannot bridge such a gap. It takes an entire community to do that. And so although that person enters into a relationship in order to satisfy his need for a community, it doesn't work. One person cannot fulfill all his needs, cannot make up for a lack of community that has been felt since birth.

It is normal and even necessary that the arrival of a newborn bring a change in the relationship of the parents. As mothers we have to build an intimate relationship with the baby while it is still in the womb and continue to nourish this relationship after birth. It is the responsibility of the father to develop a relationship with the child also. Unless both parents are closely tied to the child and, along with that, keep their relationship between each other healthy, somebody will feel left out.

After the arrival of a child, or even before its birth, a ritual should be done involving spirit and the community, welcoming the baby into the family, acknowledging the new spirit that has come, and affirming the parents' commitment to the child and to each other.

CHAPTER 6

INITIATION: GAINING KNOWLEDGE

In our village, children learn about intimacy and ritual from birth onward. As they mature, it becomes crucial that they develop a profound understanding of these matters. At initiation, elders guide the young deeper into intimacy, sexuality, and ritual so that they know what is awaiting them. They do not just wander into the unknown territory of adulthood and get wounded.

Initiation for women takes place after the first menstrual period. It is performed once a year, between December and February. If, for instance, you get your period in March, you will have to wait until the next initiation in order to go through initiation. For a man, initiation is done at puberty, when he starts to show signs of wanting to be an adult, when the hormones start to kick in.

During initiation you learn about many things; sex and intimacy are just part of the teachings. Even after initiation, there is a long period of mentoring. If you think there is something you are not grasping, you can always turn to an elder.

Intimacy is a sacred thing and should not be messed with. There is high danger in it. When you jump into it with your eyes closed, you can easily get hurt. That's why this mentoring is so important; it helps you avoid acting on illusory knowledge.

In initiation, one important lesson is learning how to build an intimate connection with spirit, the self, and others. For the Westerner, the question is usually, "How do you build a relationship with yourself, with another, or with spirit, for that matter?"

In my own case, I had to learn to let go of my defenses and any need to control. I had to trust spirit absolutely for guidance. But you know many things are easier said than done, especially when we are anxious. I remember many times when I would spit and scream and yell at spirit when I felt frustrated. But this is to be expected; it's all part of the learning process.

I particularly enjoyed the frankness and openness between the youth and adults—especially the elders. They did not hide anything from us. They talked to us about their own experiences, the kinds of difficulties they encountered in their own intimate lives, and how they were able to overcome them.

In initiation, we looked at the connection that women have with their cycles and the moon. This discussion opened something infinite in me.

Many of the civilized countries of the world, including some African countries, look at the menstruating woman with some discomfort. People ignore the sacredness of menstruation. They do not understand how valuable it is for a woman to have her period. Yet the flow of the menstrual blood carries power. It's a powerful time for the mooning woman. She carries healing energy within her and has a tremendous ability to heal and see into things. In my village, people will seek help from such a woman. They will treat her with great respect.

Women do rituals for an individual who is having her period. There is also the need for someone to contain the space for the mooning woman, as she could be channeling energies from different sources. Rituals take whatever form the menstruating woman chooses. Some women will say, "I want to be carried to this place in the village and have people sing and dance and rock me." They have no restrictions. Both men and women can be involved in these rituals, though they often involve only women. The woman having her period can ask them to do whatever she wants.

During menstruation, sacred sexuality can happen with a woman depending on the kind of energy that exists between partners. The man must work at raising his energy to match that of the woman. If not, he could suffer from such an encounter. He could become disempowered.

One elder pointed out that the risk is similar to sharing an intimate space before working on your anger. Your anger will transfer to the other person and backfire on you.

This made sense to me. I then understood why the elders insist on the need to clear a ritual space before doing anything intimate. People who think that, in this context, they can get power from a partner without being established in their own power are fooling themselves.

Throughout the initiation, we noticed the recurrence of the number 4 in different situations. When asked, the elders explained that 4 was the symbol of the woman. One elder gave a very complicated explanation for this, then added that women also have four lips.

I felt a sense of recognition, as though someone had just woken me up. I realized that on the day I had first menstrual blood, I was given a four-legged stool. I was told the meaning of it at the time and that a man would not use it if I did not give him permission to do so, but the excitement of becoming a woman clouded my ability to listen.

We went on exploring more of the mysterious dimensions of women. We talked about what Westerners would call our "private parts" and shared our deepest feelings and thoughts. We learned about the ash circle of intimacy and how to uphold this sacred space.

By the end of the session, I felt as though I had eaten something so filling that it would take me forever to digest it.

After initiation, I had to face up to the purpose I had chosen and declared before I came to this world. I was reluctant to do certain things and realized that to promise to do something before being born does not necessarily mean having the courage or the willingness to do it. The idea of leaving the village especially did not appeal to me at all. I wanted someone to delete that part of my life purpose.

Until that point, I had been quite happy with my life in the village. I hoped that the mentoring sessions that followed initiation would help me out of this dilemma. I was disappointed then to discover that nobody took the step to say, "You don't have to do it." I realized that there were difficulties involved with pursuing one's life purpose.

After initiation the elders start to look for the person you will marry. While you are being mentored—somewhere between the ages of sixteen and twenty—marriages happen.

CHAPTER 7

MARRIAGE: TWO WORLDS TOGETHER

Marriage is a way of taking the call of the spirit further. It brings two souls, two purposes, two worlds together, and allows them to bring their gifts forward to benefit the community.

Marriage is a way for spirit to bring its support for two people into one greater energy. It brings together two or many lines of ancestors, two cultures, and many different ways of looking at the world.

Marriage is two souls coming into one soul—still distinct but forming one entity. It is a way of bringing two people's gifts together in order to strengthen them and make them even better. It acknowledges that two people are embarking on something that is bigger than them and bigger than the tribe.

Marriage is a communion with all the spirit allies. It's a communion with all the gifts that two people or more are bringing together. It's a communion of the things that are at the very core of the soul.

Marriage is a renewal of vows for those who have already married. It's a way of family coming together, a way of tribes coming together, and it's an opportunity to celebrate the call that two souls or two spirits heard and answered.

When we come together as a couple, we bring two worlds together. In order to open our world to the other person, we must go through spirit. Ignoring spirit and making your marriage a private thing that is just between two individuals will bring a lot of disappointment.

In the indigenous context of Africa, the concept that each one of us comes into this world for a purpose determines who you eventually enter into a relationship with. Certain purposes are more or less similar. Some are very much alike. This is where you go and look for a possibility of a relationship.

Selecting a partner is the business of the elders, who because they know everybody in the village know everyone's purpose and are best equipped to understand who can go with whom within the community. This requires a great deal of trust and places a lot of burden on the elders. If a marriage doesn't work, they have to figure out a way to correct it through ritual.

Elders take several factors into account when making arrangements for the young initiate to marry. Marriages are not arranged randomly. If, for instance, they were to put two people together whose purposes clash, they would murder each other. The elders have to see that your energies are compatible, that you can live with each other in harmony, that your life purposes are on the same road.

In addition to that, the elders must divine on the subject to make sure that what they are proposing is meant to work. They will present the matter to spirit and do a ritual to confirm and seal spirit's approval. Then they will inform

the villages and the individuals involved in the process—
the bride and groom.

I had just completed the full cycle of initiation at the
age of sixteen when I was called into the circle of the elders,
and I was quite surprised. One can never guess why the
elders call one into their circle, but one thing is sure: their
cooking pot always has something boiling in it.

At any rate, when I got there, they said, "Well, we have
this son who lives in the West, and we need somebody
who can keep him company." My answer was "What does
that have to do with me?" And their response was "You
see, you are the kind of person who can get along with
him. We would like you to marry him." I said, "Well, isn't
there anybody else in the village who can get along with
him?"

My ambivalence about leaving the village led me to a
state of confusion, which in turn confused the elders, who
did not know what to tell me. The only thing they said
was "Your life purpose, Sobonfu, is on the same road as
his. We're not trying to force you to marry somebody,
because we know that being far away from home is very
difficult. If he lived somewhere around here, we wouldn't
have even called you here. We wouldn't have had this

meeting and given you a choice. You would have simply been notified."

So I said, "How am I going to live far away and be able to survive without my family and without everybody else?" And they said, "You are going to be taken care of. You just need to give us your yes, and then everything will be fine." And I said, "Well, I can't give you my answer right now because I don't know what I'm dealing with." So they said, "Well, you have some time. Go think about it, and come back and tell us what you think."

I thought about it for three months. First I went to my parents and said, "What do you think I should do?" They said, "No. You can't ask us. We are too attached to this issue to give you good advice." My grandmother had just passed away, and she had been my main counselor. After a month I went to my other grandmothers, and they said that they, too, were too attached to give me any kind of advice.

And so I spent some time around my grandmother's grave. One night, as I was sitting on her grave, these words came to me: "Don't worry. Just say yes, and you'll see that everything will be fine." And so the next day I woke up, and I went to the elders and said yes.

They were quite relieved, and they said, "We'll start everything, and the wedding will be on its way." I didn't know Malidoma, my future husband, but I knew his family. He was the only person in his family that I didn't know. So the wedding came when I was twenty, and since, in the village, you do not need to be at your wedding, Malidoma wasn't there. He was notified by mail afterward.

Malidoma had been sent to the West by the elders to teach their wisdom and to become, as his name describes, "a friend of the stranger." He had studied first at the University of Ouagadougou in Burkina Faso and then at the Sorbonne in France, after which he ended up in America. At the time of our wedding he was in America, at Brandeis University in Massachusetts.

Malidoma saved enough money to buy himself a ticket, and a year later he came home and we met. We were introduced as a couple. We didn't know each other, and we wondered how in the world we were going to make anything happen. Now, one of the things that I had learned from the elders in initiation was how to create a sacred space, and how to build an intimate relationship in that space. As Malidoma and I spent time together, we started to work on that issue.

In the village, women and men do not sleep together. Though they share the same compound, women sleep in their quarters, and men sleep in their quarters, and that is because, in order to bring their strength to society, they need to empower one another; they need to bring one another's best out so that whenever a woman goes out to meet with the man, there isn't an imbalance created.

The first thing that people want to know when they hear of this sleeping arrangement is how a couple manages to get together. I tell them that as long as they keep their creativity and imagination alive, they will figure it out.

Malidoma came home, and at the time I was sleeping with his mother. His mother and I used to share the same bed. You can understand how frustrating the idea of being married to a woman who sleeps with your mother can be to the Western mind. For me what was harder was being in a sacred space with Malidoma, someone I did not know. There was something strange about it. So I surrendered to spirits, letting them figure it out. All I needed to do when I felt frustrated was to create a sacred space.

The way we created sacred space in the village was just by using ash to make a circle. You bring an earthen pot full of water, and you put it in the middle of the circle. Whoever starts the ritual will sit and wait for the other person to come. When the other person gets there, then you do an invocation, and as you invoke the spirit, something inside automatically unlocks itself.

Malidoma and I were strangers to each other, but each time we met in that space, it was as if we had known each other forever.

In an indigenous context, because you don't follow romance as a guide to marriage, partners know the true identity of the other. You know the strengths and the weaknesses of the person you are going to marry. That way you won't wonder ten years down the road whether you married the right person or their ghost.

People think that when they say yes once, it means yes forever. But in the indigenous context, no. That's why you have to constantly renew your vows, whether it's once a year or when somebody else is getting married.

If a couple renew their vow at least once a year, and also are able to do ritual constantly to strengthen their connection to spirit and acknowledge each other's spirit, their marriage will never degenerate into weakness.

In the Dagara community marriage is not a private matter. It's not just two individuals getting married. In fact, when a couple gets married, they create an occasion for other people to renew their vows and to get married once again, at the same time. Sharing the wedding is a way of enlisting support for when problems start to hit.

In the West, although everybody likes going to weddings, once you call somebody and say that trouble has hit, nobody wants to show up. But in the kind of community I'm talking about, once people have shared in a couple's marriage vow, they are going to be involved in whatever is happening. When trouble hits, they will be the first ones to show up.

Marriage is two or more tribes, two villages, or at the least, two families coming together. The two people who actually join in a marriage are almost, in this grand scale, a minor incident. And so I have a strong sense that two people who come together do so not only to affirm their desire to uphold a certain tradition of community, but also because they need this relationship as an icon—a smaller piece of a much bigger sense of connectedness in their life.

Let me put it differently. I fell in love with my husband, you know, after we got married. What was important in the process was the realization that he was married not to someone named Sobonfu alone but to a whole ethnic group, a whole family, and a whole village. And that I, in the middle of that, was of course important. But my importance rested in the grander scale of the community that brought him to me.

It made me realize that I could not personalize my relationship with him. Because it's not an "I" relationship, it's a "we" relationship, and the "we" is not limited to two people but is extended to a whole village.

By voicing their commitment to marriage, a couple voices a commitment to spirit, a commitment to the self, to the other person, and to the community at large. The community, by being there and taking their vow, is doing the same, so it's mutual.

A wedding is an opportunity—an obligation almost— for everyone to reaffirm relationships with one another, with the ancestors, with all the things around. So the wedding is not just a matter between two people but an event with a purpose for everyone in the village.

Before a wedding in the village, the people who have gone through initiation with the bride and groom give the couple their blessing and their encouragement. The elders also come and give their blessing. They will add that they have traveled this same route, that it wasn't all smooth, that there are bumps along the road, and that this is okay. Hearing from the elders that the intimacy road is not paved with pearls and gold, and that you have to constantly work at it, helped remove unrealistic expectations from our marriage basket.

In our culture, in order for a couple to get married, there are a multitude of rituals that must be done. After the spirits' approval of the union, for instance, there is the transfer-of-the-two-souls ritual. There is another ritual that brings the two souls together. And there is a ritual that unites the purposes of the two people, because when you marry there is a purpose in life that you will share.

So however hard it may be to imagine someone not being at his own wedding, it works because the whole wedding is focused on spirit and ritual. If you have some object belonging to and representing the absent person, then his spirit can be brought into the ritual. It is actually there.

After the long wedding celebration, there is a welcoming ritual that functions as a bridge to incorporate the bride into the groom's family. Then, usually, one doesn't immediately spend time with her spouse—there's no honeymoon. Some of the bride's family members will stay with her to make sure she is integrating well into her new home. And the women of her new family will spend time with her and welcome her into a new women's circle, where from now on, she will be taken care of and given all the support she needs.

In Africa, gifts are exchanged before the marriage. This aspect of African culture is usually misunderstood in the West. Many people see it as the selling of the bride. It may have become so in various parts of the continent under the influence of the West and modernity, in those places where people are desperate for material goods and have lost their connection to spirit and ritual. Because their ancestors did something they no longer understand, some people try to take advantage of it however they can.

But in Dagara practice, you cannot afford to take such an advantage. Using a family member's marriage gift for personal gain brings death to the family. Some people have tried it and learned the hard way before dying. During my most recent trip home the village was upset by the death of a young man who tried to sell the cow that was given for his sister's soul-transfer ritual. When he found out that he had been caught by the ancestors, he called everybody to confess what he had done in an attempt to redeem himself. But it was too late. He said that whenever he looked around, he saw himself being beckoned by his own ghost.

No one could have imagined that such an adored young man could have been tempted in this way. It was not that he was ignorant of the danger, but the temptation of a trip to a city in the Ivory Coast just clouded his ability to see and feel his responsibilities.

When a woman marries, although she keeps her family name and passes it over to her children, she moves to her husband's family. We are thus matrilineal and patrilocal.

In order for the bride to leave her house, her soul has to be transferred from her family to her husband's. This is done by a giveaway, a sacrifice of a cow. This cow is given by the husband's family to the family of the bride. Without this transferring-of-the-soul ritual, the woman usually finds it hard to stay in her new family. Her spirit will long to go back to the place where it feels at home.

When the bride's family receives the cow, it is slaughtered, then left on the roof of the family compound as an offering to spirit. It has to be left out for at least one night for the spirit to come and feast on it, and nobody shall eat a piece until the spirit has been satisfied. So the spirit will come and inspect what it has been given and decide whether it is satisfied with the ritual. If not, on the next day you will find that the meat is inedible; this means that the sacrifice was not done properly. But if you go the next day and find that it's okay, you know that it is good, that spirit has feasted on it, and then everybody else may feast on it. The meat is first shared among everybody in the bride's family, then some of it is taken to the husband's family. It's their responsibility to share with their village.

Now, after the soul has been transferred from one house to another, there is another ritual that has to be done in order to bring the two souls together. All the family members come together. There is an invocation calling the spirits to come and oversee this union, and if there's any obstacle, the spirits are asked to clear the path for the couple, to give them their blessing and an extra eye to see, to help them with their day-to-day life. A pot made for the occasion is brought out, and the birth stones of the bride and groom are put together in it. These are the stones that were picked by them during the hearing rituals done before their birth. In addition, two pots containing each person's medicine are blessed.

Then everybody present offers a prayer for the couple, and afterward they put water in the pot with the stones. Sometimes they put additional things such as seeds and roots in it; then the pot is taken to the husband's family shrine. It will remain there for the rest of the couple's lives.

Back in the village, these two stones are together in the medicine room for the marriage of Malidoma and me. When one of us dies, a ritual of separation will allow the stones to be taken out of the pot, and the stone of the deceased person will then be placed in or on top of the grave.

These are some of the rituals associated with marriage in our culture. There are many, many more.

When people say that they get married in order to have children, the statement is too limited. It does not take into account that the two spirits who have come together have their own higher purposes. If a couple is married only in order to have children, they risk failing to fulfill their own purposes, and this failure is transferred to the child.

What I mean by this is that if two people who are married do not acknowledge that they have a higher purpose to fulfill, and limit their marriage to just having children, they put their purpose to sleep. When children finally arrive, the parents realize that there is something that they haven't been able to fulfill, and they hope their children will fulfill it for them.

This puts all the expectations of the parents onto the child, and it doesn't give the child a chance to actually take his own purpose into his own hands. Parents who think their sole purpose is to have children often have a hard time staying together after their children leave home.

In our village, polygamy is allowed. It is not viewed as adultery, because it is not hidden and is only done with the approval of the wife. It's up to the woman to choose whether she wants another woman in her household.

A second wife is wed into the family just as any other marriage. Many women choose this in order to bring more female energy into the house and make it lively. My aunt chose to have several other women with her. It's not seen as perverted. It's the action of a woman who feels happy in her relationship and wants to bring other women to share that happiness with her.

Sometimes a man will say no to multiple wives, when he knows he would be unable to sustain intimacy with more than one woman.

To keep a marriage healthy, the first thing is to honor the relationship itself. Come to it as something led by spirit.

The next step is to acknowledge each other's soul, acknowledge each other not just as human beings but as spirits who have chosen a body to come into. Then, through ritual, bring these two souls together.

Perhaps couples in the West could use meaningful things they have had since childhood, objects that have become sacred to them. With the presence of relatives or friends, bring those two sacred objects together in a pot or basket, then keep them in a space reserved as a shrine. It can be kept in the bedroom, or somewhere in the house where both can have access to it.

You can use that special place to draw energy from, especially when things become hard. You can go back to that source, access the time before problems came, and really draw energy from that.

CHAPTER 8

INTIMACY: IN THE ASH CIRCLE

When people recognize that they are spirit in a human body and that other people are spirits, they begin to understand that our bodies are sacred and that sexuality is far more than a means of pleasure; it is a sacred act. They look at other people differently, seeing the body not as a source of physical attraction but as a shrine.

Maybe the way to start on the path to a healthy intimate life is to recognize the divine in everything. When we acknowledge that the earth we walk upon is not just dirt, that the trees and animals are not just resources for our consumption, then we can begin to accept ourselves as spirits vibrating in unison with all the other spirits around us. Our connection to all these living spirits helps determine the kind of intimate life we live.

The Dagara people believe that when two people share a spirited and balanced intimate life, they have the power to raise a healing energy for everything around them. For this reason a couple might dedicate their sacred intimacy to some higher purpose, in addition to the well-being of their own relationship.

A couple's intimacy is not about the pursuit of pleasure. It is the pursuit of a kind of power that only spirit can give in a sacred context. It's not going to be found on a public road or in the village circle; it's going to be in the ash circle, in a place turned into a shrine, an altar, a sacred space. By creating a sacred space, we open ourselves to other spirits and we give ourselves permission to completely open up to another. We allow ourselves to be our true self and to be fully present.

The couple in a sacred space is there because they have first admitted that they don't know what they are doing. They move themselves into that place in order to enable spirit to come and be their teachers.

If you try to aim at pleasure only, intimacy will be short. You will get finished with it in a short time. If you can look at intimacy as spirit-driven and go beyond the limitation of pleasure, then intimacy can have a long-lasting effect. It can be life-giving and healing.

You don't wait until your hormones are taking over your body in order to bring some ash and make a circle and jump in. "Get the water in quickly!" No. You need to give yourself room to dissipate negative energy, honor each other's spirit, and give permission to each other. When you use ash, it protects you from negative energies passing by, but you must also be sure that you or your partner release any negative energy you might have carried into the ash circle. Negative thoughts are a powerful poison. They will linger around, and when we vibrate in harmony with them they come into us and take over.

So what happens is that physical attraction becomes intimidated in the ash circle. Something happens when you use the ash and speak from your heart to spirit about what is going to take place. The intimate focus stops being caused by sexual impulse and becomes channeled by spirits.

Whatever attraction you were feeling becomes something else.

All of a sudden you realize that you are involved in a situation that is a lot greater than who you are. It is not going to be a context in which two people interact. There may be quite a few spirits who are showing the road, guiding the way, whom you need first to officially bring in. That invitation must be expressed to them in terms of our inability to carry out anything sacred by ourselves and our need to be enabled.

The Dagara people do not have a specific word for sex. We express the concept of sex in terms of journeying or traveling with someone. You don't want to have sex with that person; you want to go somewhere. And usually that place is not known by you or by your partner. But you know someone who knows it—either the spirit of your grandfather, your ancestors, your dog, your cat, or some kind of spirit that you have encountered in the course of your life.

So you call in those spirits; they become the horse on the back of which that journey can happen. And that horse is going to take you wherever it has plotted to take you, so that you have the learning or the vision that always comes in the context of intimacy.

In a genuine intimate situation, the visual and the spiritual horizon increases. There is no sense of confinement. There is even a postponement of anything pleasurable about it. It's about a total evaporation of the conscious eye and jumping into a very dynamic collective space. Somehow the intimate relationship becomes an icon of the intimate relationship between the tribal community and its ancestors, and between you as a person and the tribal communities to which you belong.

Any attempt at moving into that place by accepting an aesthetic invitation—presented by someone with a certain kind of pleasing appearance, for instance—is in fact a danger. Most people fall prey to aesthetic delusion because of their lack of spiritual groundedness. When you get caught in that, it is like eating ice cream that has poison in it. As you eat the first cup, it tastes good. The second one tastes pretty good. Then you forget. And the next bite becomes lethal.

This is why children, from the beginning, are always warned about the danger of jumping into this type of ritual space without prior guidance. Children are taught to look at that kind of journey with a lot of caution, because there is the danger of not being able to return from where they are taken. This is why, when adolescents are ready for initiation, people know that their hormones are starting to pull them toward an unknown place. Initiation is a reversal of that process, in the course of which the ritual space is unveiled. It is a time where they are taught to use their sexual energy for a higher purpose and to direct it toward spirit and healing.

In a sacred space, any bad feelings that you have toward your partner must be resolved. Also, any kind of control issues have to be dropped, because the more you try to control the situation, the more you will harm the other person. Your partner will start to feel distant from you, and the relationship will become a one-way street.

As a couple grows together, the merging of their souls will eventually give birth to a new spirit. The birth of that spirit comes as a direct result of the couple fully embracing their intimacy. You can tell whether this is happening by watching what they do outside. Soon enough you may see a tendency for one or the other to be sexually interested in another person somewhere else. This is seen as extremely dangerous.

Because of the kind of bonding ritual that my husband

and I have done, if I were to go out and have an affair, come back home, and give my husband something and he puts it into his body, or if I meet him in an intimate space again, he can't live. He will die.

You see, when a couple is bound and has joined at a deep and spiritual level, their energy resembles that of one person. So when one person is unfaithful, the purity of the ancestry is stained, an alien energy has been brought in that injures the other. The wound is as deep as the depth of their intimacy and can be fatal. This is why people who separate from their partners have so much grief and pain.

In many villages in Africa, the intrusion of the modern world, which sends young married men into the city while their wives and children are still at home, has caused a whole series of bad events. Those who have left for the city get involved with other relationships there. When they return home, they think that other relationship happened far away, it never happened in the village. They forget about their spouse's spirit and think that they can get away with it. Before anybody can do anything about the situation, someone is dead. The same thing happens in the West, when the pain of adultery kills or breaks the heart of loved ones.

Sexuality is so complicated in the West! When Westerners come to the village, they see men and women relating to each other in a much different way. If they were to see a woman walking with her breasts uncovered in downtown San Francisco, they would stop and wonder if it's an open invitation to sex, and if so, who it is meant for, and all these other things. But in the village, women always walk around without any top. It's absolutely fine. You won't see anybody say, "This woman is crazy!" or jump on her because she is so attractive.

A different vision of sexuality is hard for Westerners to understand because the issue is not addressed, not spoken of frankly here. It is a sensitive subject. That is why you have infidelity, because it's so mysterious. Nobody tells how it really feels. Everyone wonders, and soon everyone wants to try it and see how it feels for themselves.

In a culture where sexuality is not honored as sacred, to fully embrace one's sexuality means to work against the grain. Shame, self-consciousness, and self-doubt are always lingering around, ready to knock on the door of the psyche. Many people find it so frightening that they live in denial of their sexuality.

Shame is so big in Western culture that it oppresses everybody. Ritual can help us to accept ourselves and accept our spirit as a way to free sexual blockages.

Teaching children about intimacy and encouraging them to embrace it instead of hiding it from them would take away a lot of the shame and confusion that the West is experiencing. Shame arises simply because adults aren't telling their children the truth about sexuality, and when they discover this "forbidden fruit," they're punished. There is a need for teaching them that intimacy is about spirit, not just about some one-night stand, before they reach the age of dealing with these things.

Before coming to America, I took it for granted that everybody knew how to dance. When people asked me to teach dance steps, I was surprised. At any rate, I was asked to teach some teenagers how to dance, and when I instructed them to move their hips a certain way, they resisted. They that thought it was "dirty" to move that way. From an African point of view I did not see anything wrong with it. It is a way of moving sexual energy, of embracing one's own sexuality and also of unblocking repressed sexual energies. I later found out that just moving the hips was seen as very provocative in this country and that a person who did such things should be ashamed.

In the village, any public display of intimacy is seen as a display of power and therefore makes a couple vulnerable to all sorts of outside forces. The more it is openly displayed, the more its power will be drained out. Intimate life, when opened to spectators, is sure to decline. Spectators create a leak that kills the very spirit we are trying to cultivate.

I was taught that intimacy is a ritual and must happen inside ritual or sacred space. Intimacy outside this space is lethal.

No one can feel sexually who does not have in his or her bones something sacred. It's a very hard concept to explain, but the point is that there is an intimate connection between sex and the sacred. A person who is desperately drawn to sexual activity is in a lot of ways a person who is desperately trying to break into the spirit world. He thinks that the more he involves himself in sexual activity, the more he will find himself or find spirit.

It never happens this way, because it is done outside of a sacred context. However, his desire indicates a deeply rooted belief that something greater is there. And I think that this is another sign that it is impossible to separate or disassociate our lives from the sacred.

We all have something in common, which is the craving for intimacy. Intimacy is a sacred thing. This is why I think that modern culture, in its advertising of sex, is actually in a misguided fashion advertising its longing for the sacred. If you accept that what everybody is craving is something sacred and you see this huge billboard with all kinds of attractive sexual images, then behind that you can see a psyche longing to reconnect with something it knows has the power to heal.

So, in the midst of that, what can you do? First you have to look at intimacy as an alignment between the self and the sacred, look at your intimate life as a communion with the sacred. If you understand that, then you can see in the practice of sexuality something that is essentially ritualistic.

CHAPTER 9

THE ILLUSION OF ROMANCE

Romantic love is an attraction that cuts off spirit and community, leaving two people to invent a relationship by themselves. It is the opposite of a relationship that lets spirit be the guide.

Romance ignores all the stages of a spiritual coming together, where we begin at the bottom of the mountain and gradually travel in unison to the top. It does not leave room for the true identity of the people involved to show through. It fosters anonymity and forces people to masquerade.

Before I was married, I didn't look at young men in the village with romantic or sexual interest. You have to understand that in the village, there is a different way of seeing people. People aren't viewed as sources of sexual attraction. People are looked at primarily as brothers, sisters, friends. We have good relationships with the opposite sex without any kind of sexual feeling. Girls and boys grow appreciating one another as spirits, as brothers and sisters, without the interference of sexuality. That's how people are brought up in the village.

The elders teach that if our relationship with people around us is focused on sexual attraction, it diminishes our capacity for friendship and our eyes will not allow us to see others as they really are.

Today in the cities of West Africa you will see the same romantic kind of love that you see here. The influence of television and movies is everywhere. Young people in the city believe that's the way of the West. And since they've been to school, they have to prove that they are civilized; they have to do it the way of the civilized.

The elders' wisdom of working from the bottom of the mountain to the top means that you make sure the other person understands who you are and you understand who the other person is every step of the way. You learn which areas make your partner scream and what makes your partner laugh—things like that.

The elders know that if you start the relationship off

with romance, more often than not many things are covered up, and it will take years to find the true identity of your partner. That is, if you are given the chance. I know that some people live their whole life with a stranger.

Romantic love doesn't really fit in the village. It just doesn't work. The kind of passion, the kind of emotion and connection that Westerners look for from a romantic relationship, village people look for from spirit. The power of romantic love in the West is really a symptom of a separation from the spiritual.

So the romantic, if you want to use that word, is with the spirit. If a man invites a woman into ritual space, or if a woman invites a man, perhaps that's what someone would see as romantic in the village. But it's not like, "I'll take you on a trip" or something like that. No. The basic attraction is toward spirit.

You cannot take away from marriage or intimacy the presence of spirit as the guide who approves all the blessings that the elders and the community give. Romance, in that sense, has a different look from what indigenous people seek in a relationship.

In the village, we give because we want to give, and there is no going away and separating ourselves in a retreat of romance. Instead we are encouraged to expand and share our gifts as a couple within the community.

In the village, desire and lust are seen as messages brought into you from a spiritual source. If that drives you into disorderly conduct, that's where you spoil the invitation that spirit is implanting within you.

The person who feels this kind of urge needs to find out, first, where the source is. Not by looking at the other gender with sexual thoughts, but by becoming aware of the weakness that being locked on to by spirit reveals. It doesn't mean that your hormones are making you do something. Something else is going on. That's the part you need to listen to.

This is why intimacy has to be looked at ritualistically. This desire is desire to be on a journey with spirit. It is as though a horse has come in and wants you to go somewhere. Now you have to find out, where is that horse? How is it configured? And what should you do in order to mount that horse without breaking your neck?

Romance, as I understand it, is this path of coming together that leads to a honeymoon. During the crazy honeymoon, impossible promises are made. When you return home, you discover there is no way on earth these promises can be fulfilled, and so you brace yourself and hope all will work out. Then things start to fall apart. This is what I call the honeymoon suicide.

Romance means hiding our true self in order to gain acceptance. It begins with doing every little thing for our partner, neglecting our true feelings, until we reach a point of serious depletion.

It would have been better from the beginning to say, "I can give you this much, that's how far I can go. With your help, I might be able to go farther, but I won't give you a false image of myself." Without this kind of honesty, our partner is left to wonder, "Wow, is this the same person I married?" He is left to pull out his hair and wonder if he is sane or his partner is insane.

If a relationship is based on a one-way street, the person at the receiving end will do all he can to get his bottomless hole fed, not caring about what happens to his partner. That kind of person does not even care whether his partner lives or dies. He married Mrs. Perfect so that he could be taken care of and is not ready to have that change.

People in the West must always remember that the energy they vibrate sends a message that only certain people will respond to. They must make their intention clear while looking for someone, and they must keep their clarity once an intimate relationship is established. They must constantly check themselves to make sure they are staying in alignment with their true selves.

The kind of attitude people have when initiating a relationship will determine what happens later. And if there is something unspoken, it will usually lead to the death of the relationship.

If, for instance, your partner is holding something back and thinking, "If I show this part of myself, then she is going to get scared and run away," well, he can be sure you will someday run away.

Openness is needed from the beginning so that people know what they are getting into. Being very nice, you know, is not always the right way.

CHAPTER 10

CONTINUAL RENEWAL

There is a need to periodically cleanse our relationship with our partner. There is always something in the self that is either overcompensating, pretending, giving in, or pushing too hard. The only way one can reach that and move it out is through a ritual.

Before we can communicate in deeper states of intimacy, we must address the subtle things that our partner has done that we didn't like. Because of some rule of gentility, we tend not to respond to them and they pile up. Our thoughts take us to places of uncertainty and the postponement of confrontation, and then we become very passive. It is fine to be polite, but where is the place for us to speak our frustration and disappointment?

In ritual, such politeness may be put aside. Once you have drawn a line marking sacred space and called upon spirit, there is no lying, no pretending. In this space it is sometimes best even to shout your frustrations, because what you're saying is so real.

In our village, every five days there is an opportunity for renewal of a relationship, on a day chosen by the couple. All the bad things that the couple has accumulated are ejected. Usually the woman sits facing north, back-to-back with the man, who sits facing south, within a circle of ash. The ritual starts with an invocation of spirit. Then the two people start to express aloud, to spirit, their frustrations. As they do so their pain increases, then explodes. Each person is busy speaking his own pain and does not pay attention to what the other is saying. Some people whisper, some people shout, some people prefer other ways of communication. It is up to the individuals involved to decide what is best for them, as long as they are using methods that enable them to release all of their feelings. In our village, there is usually a lot of gesticulation to allow the body to speak. This is not, however, an opportunity to get into a fistfight.

If outsiders were to observe this ritual, they might fear

that the couple were going to kill each other. But if they watch long enough, they will see that the ritual has a powerful, emotional ending. The couple will slow down, reach a reconciliation, and then pour water onto each other. The heart of this process is washing away all the friction that has settled into the couple's life.

Think of this ritual not as a confrontation but as a renewal of the marriage vow. In Dagara culture we don't believe that saying yes one time is enough for intimacy to always be there. We need to renew our intimacy continuously and make it as close to what spirit wants as possible.

This ritual of renewal can also be good for people who have a history of time limits for their relationships, who are able to be in a relationship for only, let's say, a year or so, then they have to get out. Renewing their commitment before that time limit arrives can be helpful in breaking this pattern. It helps because some people can get really caught up in telling themselves that all their relationships are temporary.

Outside of ritual, there is a tendency is to blame the other person. We don't see our own actions. Creating a ritual space to release tensions helps us be open to our partner's concerns, and it creates in us an ear that can listen without being defensive.

Sometimes our partner may offend us without even realizing it. Maybe something was going on inside him, and we just happened to be the nearest person to strike out at. We do not usually mean to hurt our loved ones, but in times of pressure it can happen.

The renewal ritual gives us an opportunity to heal those wounds and hurts. It creates a space where couples can voice their hurts without placing blame and pointing fingers. There is simple power in voicing things; it helps people let go of them. And when water is applied at the end of the ritual, it rinses them away and brings about peace in the relationship.

The renewal ritual can be performed by two people without the presence of the community. It is an important ritual in the sense that it allows couples to clear the air before jumping into sexual intimacy. If you carry anger or sadness into intimacy, you will transfer that energy to your partner.

Unless the problems in a relationship are really huge, this ritual prevents small issues from piling on top of one another to become big issues. When we don't listen to the little things happening around us, we end up having huge earthquakes. So this kind of renewal and cleansing of a relationship is very important to intimate life, especially for newly wed couples.

Whenever a couple renews their relationship, an alignment of spirits takes place. Special powers come out of this alignment. Remember that this is not just about the spirits of two people. We are talking about the spirits of a whole village or a whole tribe coming into alignment; the power that comes out of that is healing.

In the village, there are all kinds of rituals done around the issue of renewal. There are every-day and every-five-day renewal rituals done by the couple. There is also a yearly atonement ritual that is a communal ritual, with its focus on the couples. It helps people be concerned about other people's problems.

In Africa they say that if one person gets sick, everybody is sick. The village or the tribe is seen as a huge tree with thousands of branches. When a part of this living entity is diseased there is a need to reexamine the whole tree. This is why when somebody is sick in the village, everybody is worried; it reminds everybody that there is something present that is potentially dangerous for all.

When people hear that something bad happened to somebody, they don't say, "I'm glad it's not me." Instead they bring their support to help this person gain peace again. It is for this reason that the yearly atonement ritual to heal couples' differences and wounds and to restore peace is done as a community.

The elders will set a date for all the couples in the village to meet at the riverbank. Each couple will bring along with them the two pots that were made for their wedding. These small pots were blessed at that time, one for each person, and are kept in their shrines. In each of these jars there is a talisman, as well as medicines, herbs, water, and other things. After the invocation, each couple steps forward and hands their jars to the elders. The elders mix together a little bit of the water from each pot. The water is then presented to each person to sip or cleanse the body with. If they take the medicine, it means that they have agreed to resolve their differences. If they don't, another problem is created and the elders must find out what is happening. This is rare, since such conflicts are usually taken care of in a community ash circle before the atonement ritual begins.

Then each couple is taken to the river, where the women of the village will bathe the woman and then walk her to a specific place to await her partner. The men will do the same simultaneously for the man, leaving a distance between him and his wife. As people sing a special journeying song to the couple, they go under the water and manage to meet there. When they come out holding hands, you will hear a lot of screaming and yelling in the village. This means that spirits have once again given their blessing to the couple's journey.

Without completely getting out of the water, the couple will then make a vow to spirit, to each other, to the community, and to all the natural forces around them—earth, water, mountains, creeks, animal, rocks, fire, trees, and so forth. Renewal rituals do not limit themselves to people. People renew their relationship with everything around them. They need to have a good relationship with all these things in order to make their relationship work. At the end they thank them for their help.

After this atonement ritual, which ends with many days of celebration, I can't wait for next year's ritual. I imagine myself going crazy without it. As people go home filled with the spirit of renewal, they commit themselves more than ever to working on their intimate life. Everybody wants to keep their relationship healthy.

There are many opportunities in the West to be in rituals with friends and family members. These are people we need to renew our vows with, too. The rituals can be either celebratory or designed to clear the air.

Family reunions would have a different taste if they were given such new meanings. They could become a time when each individual is seen and acknowledged by the family as a whole. Family members would be more supportive of one another if they created rituals in which they could express their continuing support for one another or work at bridging differences.

Those who attended the marriage ceremony should be the first to see where a couple is not strong enough, and help them be strong. They should periodically bring them to a ritual where they can look at their weaknesses, acknowledge them, and take steps toward strengthening.

They should also bring them into rituals where they will be helped to see their best parts, their positive sides and their strengths, in order to help maintain them or even make them better. Because when two people live together, they don't necessarily always see each other's good qualities. Somebody else often has a better eye.

CHAPTER 11

CONFLICT: A SPIRIT GIFT

Conflict grows out of challenges that are presented by spirit. It is a gift, meant to help us move forward. It is through conflict that we gain knowledge of ourselves and learn new situations for using our own gifts.

Conflict is a wake-up call sent by spirit to remind us of the purpose we are here to fulfill. In an indigenous context, it is seen as a blessing. It should not be nurtured; it should be listened to, and proper steps should be taken to address the spirit behind the conflict.

Two humans together are always prone and vulnerable to some form of conflict or other. Without conflict everything is going to look pretty boring. But dwelling in conflict will make everything pretty sour. So there is a need for a constant balancing, and the ingredient for that balancing is ritual.

Ritual acknowledges that the relationship of two people is an energy higher than the two of them simply added together. It is something so big that their intellect and their own dexterity cannot handle crises that arise without the intervention of something ritualistically grounding.

When conflict shows up we may think that the best way to deal with it is to adopt an antagonistic stance toward the other person. But actually it is best to come together and tell spirit, "We've heard the words that you sent to us. We may not know what to make of them, they are very hard, very painful for us to deal with. But we understand that it is through this trial that we will find our gifts and our wisdom. Next time, if you can, make it a little less hard, it will be really helpful, because this one took a huge toll on our relationship. But we are listening, and we are willing to get beyond our resistance."

Conflict usually comes when things start to stagnate, when our ego and controlling self start to take over our relationship. Conflict is a notice that spiritual energy is being stopped and needs to move.

In the village people are encouraged to deal with conflict instead of running away from it. If they are not able to deal with it, it must be opened to the community.

Let's say, for instance, that something is really bothering a woman in the village but she is unable to speak to her husband about it. She can let her women's circle know, "This is what's aching me," and the women might speak to her husband. If he doesn't respond, all the family members—both the woman's and the man's—will be called together. If no solution is found, then the whole village will be alerted. By then you know that it's really late. Things have gotten pretty bad. It's no longer a couple problem, it's a village problem. The couple needs to stand back and let the village deal with it.

This process, with the whole community trying to help, makes it impossible for the husband to come back with serious anger at his wife for telling everyone that things aren't working. And reaching out to a larger community for a solution makes it impossible for the problem to continue.

I must point out here that there is a difference between making a relationship problem public in order to find a solution for it and making it public without wanting any kind of help. Sometimes we become accustomed to our problems and want to nourish them and not let them go. We give them room to grow, and we do not want them to get out of our life. They become a burden to those who hear about them, not knowing how to respond.

This is a modern way of getting attention. Sometimes the best medicine for people seeking this kind of attention is not to give them any energy.

Our fear of being exposed in a culture where everybody else is wearing a mask can be a major obstacle to our reaching out for help. This is why it is so crucial to have a trusted circle of people who can give you that sense of belonging and of community.

There are many ways of communicating problems to those who can help us. Some people, for instance, are very gifted in their ability to communicate through dreams and can use it as a way to connect with others. People who know us and care about us usually have an open channel for us at all times. If we are clear in our message, however we send it, they can send us the kind of help we are looking for.

In Dagara culture, water is a key element in conflict resolution because of its reconciling, unifying, and peaceful qualities. In any ritual pertaining to peacemaking or reconciliation, a lot of water is required in order for people to be brought back to a still place, to a place of alignment and serenity.

A radical conflict ritual might involve complete submersion into very cold water after an intense emotional release. In a maintenance type of ritual, one can simply use a splash of water or spend time near water.

When a couple in the village has been in serious crisis, they need a radical community ritual to separate them from the problem and bring them back together.

First the people in the village create a sacred space near a body of water; then they state the purpose of the ritual in an invocation of spirit, making their intention clear. They explain in detail how the couple has been experiencing a problem and the kinds of things they would like to see happen in the ritual. They ask spirit to come be the driver, to bring some clarity, and to open their hearts so they can listen. They ask for groundedness in order for the conflict to be dissolved and transformed into something good. The couple is then asked to share in their own words how they have been affected by the message spirit has sent them through their crisis. The source of their crisis is then released into a fire.

One at a time, each partner will then step into the water and be submerged by people of the same gender. While all of this is taking place, other people are singing and dancing on the shore to stir up energy, thus preventing stagnating energy from coming in. As the couple comes out of the water, everybody welcomes them back into the community. The ritual ends with a thanking of spirit for the good that came out of the ritual.

Another ritual of conflict resolution involves the ash circle. It is performed on behalf of a couple or for anyone in the village who is in conflict with others. It is useful in getting to the heart of village problems and eliminating the possibility of denial. If you are used to keeping your problems private, you will find this ritual extremely uncomfortable. It leaves nowhere to hide.

First the community prepares a sacred space with a circle of ash at its center. The ancestors and spirits are called upon. Then the person who asked for the ritual steps into the ash circle and calls in the person with whom he or she has something to resolve. They sit face-to-face and bow to each other before speaking. Then they speak about their conflicts and feelings, without blaming each other.

People sitting outside of the circle have the duty to speak also, if they can help bring clarity and truth without taking sides or trying divide the couple. As they hear something they need to respond to, they may enter the circle and give voice to their thoughts. Once they have done so, they must remain there until the end of the ritual. At the end, there may be ten or more people in the circle.

This ritual helps bring two people closer together by getting to the bottom of their problem without letting their emotions and suffering interfere with the process. I say this because people in the West have a tendency to bring the courthouse to this ash circle. But it is not about assigning guilt or showing one's ability to cross-examine. It is not about winning, nor is it about talking nonsense.

It requires us to speak through our heart; the logic of

the mind is an obstacle to its success. In the village it is quickly called off if the people in the middle are not willing to speak the truth.

However difficult this ritual might become, people will stay with it until clarity is brought to the group. Then water is offered to everybody to bring a general peace. Everybody bows at the end to acknowledge one another and to mark a closing.

They say that trouble becomes scared when voiced. When you talk about problems, these problems start to hate you, and usually we are safe if a problem hates us. This is one reason why, in the indigenous context, people don't mind verbalizing what is troubling them. They know that even if people don't know how to fix it right away, the simple fact that a problem has been wrapped in words can scare it away.

Even if in the West we don't have communities of the type that exist in the indigenous world, we still have circles of friends, people whom we trust, people who will respond to our call for help. So instead of calling them next weekend for a barbecue, we can call them to sit in a ritual space with us. That might mean that we spend an afternoon with them getting the material ready and making a ritual space. Then we can start calling in spirit, explaining the problem we are trying to solve. Even those who are new to ritual, if they have been involved in the preparation of the ritual space, will discover that they have become firmly established in a ritual state.

We think we give a lot of time to working out relationship problems, but maybe it's a wrong time given. We need to rethink the manner in which we invest time dealing with our problems. Perhaps it is the mind's manipulative tendency that makes us believe that when there's a problem, if we can't figure out the solution, it's because we're not imaginative enough, we don't think enough, or worse, we are worthless.

But maybe it is because we don't feel enough! If we allow the heart to approach the problems that we experience, the heart will lead us to places that are not logical, that are more effective in handling the problem. One of the heart's illogical paths is to create a ritual space and to start shouting, "Hey, I'm in trouble!"

So we need to allow ourselves to let go, to release our

problem from the grip of our mind. Only after doing so can we see things from a different perspective, from a perspective that gives strength. Otherwise we keep shrinking, becoming smaller, while the problem becomes bigger.

When problems arise, we tend to forget about the strong foundation we have in our relationship. It is helpful to go back to the time when you and your partner came together, when spirit brought you together. Remember where and when you felt the strongest, the closest and the most intimate. When you are at the lowest point of your relationship, you can have that as a frame of reference. See the language of the current problem from that angle, and you will find a way to take the relationship forward.

People come together because there is a strong moment that binds them. And that strong moment must be held, so that in the midst of crisis it can be one's principal ally. The problem is that when people are in crisis they forget that they were once strong, because they are overwhelmed. But more often than not, the crisis is like a little rat who's running around everywhere looking like a huge giant. If you have a good flashlight and you lock on to it, you realize that it's just a tiny little thing.

You will be surprised what the blessing of a community, of a circle of friends, can do for you at the end of any crisis.

CHAPTER 12

DIVORCE AND LOSS: CUTTING THE VINE

The growth of a relationship is enhanced by constant compromise, letting go, and healing. You notice the small difficulties and remove them from your way. By doing so you reaffirm the larger scale. Small difficulties are just distractions in your forward path. This understanding is one of the reasons why relationships are approached so differently in the village; it's also, perhaps, why in the Dagara language there is still no word for divorce.

In the village, marriage between two people is like entering into a house with no exit. That's not the case in the modern world. There are so many options. If something doesn't work, change it. A situation stinks, go somewhere else. The multiplicity of options prevents people from dealing with the issues that could have made them grow.

However attractive options are, this is their shadow side. They often hide the best choice, which is to stand up to things.

One might argue that this is freedom of choice. But many of the choices we face are offered by people who like to get others into trouble or are still trying to define themselves. Many terrible decisions have been made on behalf of freedom of choice.

In sacred matters such as relationships, how free are we when we cannot build the kind of relationship we want? How free when we cannot belong to what we want to belong to?

Many couples in the West will break up rather than deal with certain problems. Unresolved problems do not just disappear because we walk away. They will show up under a different face in our next relationship. Every time we move on, we take the ills of past relationships with us to the next one, until we finally wake up, bring closure to the problem, and begin the healing process.

There isn't divorce in the village because of the way people see things. People there cannot conceive of intimacy or marriage outside of their spirituality, without the guidance of spirit.

When you have a spiritual base and the support of friends and family, things work in such a way that the couple is constantly held and given energy. They have enough support to draw strength from. They are not just defending their limited resources.

Divorce is a foreign concept in the village. But in the cities of Africa, it is a serious social issue. People in the cities do not marry because they have a tradition to uphold or because they have a purpose to achieve. They do not seek spirit's blessing. There isn't the focus on the gift that would come out of such an intimate relationship. They have lost the ways of their ancestors.

Villagers takes all these matters very seriously to heart. Also, because the elders arrange marriages, it takes the pressure off the two people. They don't have to be totally responsible for their relationship; everybody shares responsibility. Their relationship has to thrive for the village to benefit from its gift, and so the whole village takes it personally when the couple is suffering. People will do anything in their capacity to make the relationship work.

The absence of this kind of support in the West contributes to divorce. There is only so much two people can do to hold their own against even the usual number of problems.

Many factors contribute to the frequency of divorce in the West—money, job conflicts, infidelity, anonymity, isolation. These result from a lack of spirit's blessing and of community support. In the village, these are not issues.

You have to go back to the fact that everything in the village, including money, is spirit-based. It is only when money is taken out of its spiritual context that it becomes this huge giant that we have to struggle with. Money was originally intended for spiritual usage. It was taken to shrines and placed there as an offering. It wasn't used as a source of power.

It's when we start to disconnect money from its original meaning that we disconnect it from spirit. Then we start to use it as a source of power. Just like intimacy. When we disconnect it from its spiritual base, we cut off its roots, and it becomes this vague thing just floating around without any kind of focus.

In the absence of spirit, money becomes connected to "mine" and "I" and if it's mine, it's not yours. It does not belong to the community and does not have anything to do with spirit.

People make money into a personal thing. It becomes all negative power and no spirit, giving it so much more energy than what it has in reality. In this case it can only become an obstacle that divides people.

In a place where spirit has been forgotten, a true sense of identity is likely to be missing. And since we have to have an identity beyond our social security number, people base their identity on their work. Many people cannot separate their identity from what they do in their professional life.

But when you have a true sense of identity, you don't feel insecure about sharing what you have. And you will never find yourself fighting over the demands of a job.

When someone dies, there is a need to separate her energy from her surviving partner. You have to undo the union of their spirits. When that is not done, there will be all kinds of problems for the survivor. He will experience a great loss of strength, and it becomes really hard for him to get himself back together. There must be an acknowledgment that death has taken place and that the other person does not have a body anymore.

It is, in a way, like when a woman gives birth. The woman and the baby have been bound together at a physical and spiritual level. Now the umbilical cord needs to be cut for the baby to survive on her own and for the mother to replenish herself. When the umbilical cord is cut, it does not mean that the bond between mother and baby is gone. They continue to bond, but the baby's life-support source changes in order for it to survive.

When one partner dies and there isn't a ritual to separate the couple's energy, it means that although the dead partner has crossed over, the spouse still has to deal with the energy of their intimacy as if he or she was alive. This can be very disruptive, even deadly, because the energy is not moving at the other end.

It is very important for a surviving partner to release every ounce of grief she feels at the funeral. Grieving is not synonymous with being weak. It is a source of strength, love, and power. It is a sign that the relationship had something valuable and irreplaceable in it.

In the tribe, a funeral lasts for seventy-two hours, and afterward a friend always takes the mourning spouse home and nurtures her soul, making sure she is doing okay. Meanwhile, other people go and clean the whole house. The house has to be renewed. All the clothes and belongings of the deceased are given away. And a coming-home ritual is done for the surviving partner, to reestablish her.

A separation ritual might involve symbolically breaking or cutting something to represent the end of the physical connection between the person who has died and the person who is still alive. The surviving partner can tell the story of how they met, how spirit got them together, the kind of spirit that came out of their wedding, about the rituals of marriage, the story of how it began and how it ended and how they feel at the moment. Is there a void?

The community members, friends, and family can also share their memories of the deceased and describe the kind of spirit that guided their relationship and how special the departed one has been for them. They then acknowledge the separation and that the physical part is over.

After the acknowledgment they can welcome the surviving partner back home—as one who has lost his mate and yet is still communing with her in the spirit form, as someone in the process of regathering his energy. It is the beginning of a new life.

When the grieving is complete and the umbilical cord between partners has been ritually cut, there is still a connection. The spirit of the dead person will always be with the survivor. But it will be present in a way that it will be beneficial to both parties.

People in the West are often fearful about letting go of a departed one. They are afraid that without the presence of the body, they will not be able to relate to the deceased again. But this would be so only if a person did not connect with the loved one at the spirit level before his or her death. Although the body goes away, the spirit always remains.

In the West, a separation ritual can be helpful in the case of divorce. Sometimes souls, when they're brought together, commune at such a deep level that if the couple do not decisively acknowledge the split in this way, it's hard for them to keep going.

In an indigenous context, to symbolize the separation of a couple by death we might use a half-dead vine, a branch on which half the leaves are still green and those at the other end are dead. At the place where they meet, the vine will be cut. This can be done in the West, too.

In the case of divorce you might use an all-living vine and cut it in half—a living vine because both people are still alive. Each person might then take a half vine and actually grow it at home.

In the village, people can remarry after their partner dies. They may do so after all the separation rituals have been completed and time has been given to them to mourn and feel the void that the death of the partner has created.

In the West, there is a tendency to fill that void with someone else quickly. This does not give a person time to sort things out. The same applies to broken relationships and divorce. But in the village, there is a period of one year during which the person goes through many separation rituals. Throughout this time, mourners are closely supported by the community so they don't mourn themselves into depression or death. At the end of the year, they cut off all their hair and give away all the clothes that they have worn during the mourning period. In the West, a survivor might adapt this ritual by symbolically cutting part of his or her hair.

Dagara people believe that hair is our antenna. We receive messages through our hair. A person cuts off hair in order to let go of something old that no longer serves her or to help her start a new life without interference from old habits.

After the hair is shaved—if, for instance, it's a woman who is still alive—the women give her a shower and then do a welcoming ritual. Then she will go back to her family. The husband's family will always go ask for her hand again and invite her to come back to their compound. She has the choice of returning or not. Only then, at the completion of these separation rituals, is she free to remarry.

When we start a relationship, it is acknowledged in so many ways—by ourselves, by our friends and community. When our partner dies or we are divorced, there has to be an acknowledgment to that effect also. We have to bring completion to our relationships.

The relationship must change and take on a new dimension. People need rituals in order to release themselves, regather themselves, and replenish their strength. This is the way for spirit to begin moving through them again.

CHAPTER 13

HOMOSEXUALITY: THE GATEKEEPERS

The words *gay* and *lesbian* do not exist in the village, but there is the word *gatekeeper*. Gatekeepers are people who live a life at the edge between two worlds—the world of the village and the world of spirit. Though they do not marry in this world, they say they have partners in other dimensions.

What they do, they don't like to communicate to anyone. It is their right to keep it to themselves. Everybody in the village respects that because without gatekeepers, there is no access to other worlds. Most people in the West define themselves and others by sexual orientation. This way of looking at gatekeepers will kill the spirit of the gatekeeper. Gatekeepers in the village are able to do their job simply because of strong spiritual connection, and also their ability to direct their sexual energy not to other people but to spirit.

The gatekeepers stand on the threshold of the gender line. They are mediators between the two genders. They make sure that there is peace and balance between women and men. If the two genders are in conflict and the whole village is caught in it, the gatekeepers are the ones to bring peace. Gatekeepers do not take sides. They simply act as "the sword of truth and integrity."

There are many gates that link a village to other worlds. The only people who have access to all these gates are the gatekeepers. I should mention here that there are two different kinds of gatekeeper.

The first group has the ability to guard a limited number of gates to the other world, specifically, those that correspond to the Dagara cosmology—water, earth, fire, mineral, and nature—because they vibrate the energies of those gates.

The second group of gatekeepers, which is our focus here, has the responsibility of overseeing all the gates. They are in contact not only with the elemental gates but also with many others. They have one foot in all the other worlds and the other foot here. This is why the vibration of their body is totally different from others. They also have access to other-dimensional entities such as the *kontombile*, small beings who are very magical and knowledgeable. They are known as leprechauns in the Irish tradition.

Now, what would happen if you're dealing with a culture that doesn't care about these gateways? What happens is that a gay person cannot do his job. Gatekeepers are left unable to accomplish their purpose. This is one of the most distinguishing factors about gays in the village. Now, as to their sexual orientation, nobody cares about this question; they care only about their performance as gatekeepers. I figure if they want people in the village to know about their sexuality, they will share it with them. I once heard that one of the reasons why gatekeepers are able to open gates to other dimensions is in the way they use their sexual energy. Their ability to focus their sexual energy in a particular way allows them to open and close different gates.

The life of gay people in the West is in many ways a reaction to pressure from a society that rejects them. This is partly because a culture that has forgotten so much about itself will displace certain groups of people, such as the gay community, from their true roles.

In the village they are not seen as the other. They are not forced to create a separate community in order to survive. People do not put a negative label on them; they are regarded no differently than any other child of the village. They are born gatekeepers, with specific purposes, and are encouraged to fulfill the role they're born to in the interests of the community.

In the village, gatekeepers have an eye on both genders. They can help the genders to understand each other better than usual in their daily life. That's why a group of women, for example, might gather and bring a male gatekeeper to help them understand certain village issues. The same thing happens on the other side, with a female gatekeeper coming into the middle of the men's circle.

In the village homosexuality is seen very differently than it is seen in the West, in part because all sexuality is spiritually based. Taken away from its spiritual context, it becomes a source of controversy and can be exploited. In the village, you would never see gatekeepers, or anybody for that matter, displaying their sexuality or commenting on the sexuality of others.

Gatekeepers hold the keys to other dimensions. They maintain a certain alignment between the spirit world and the world of the village. Without them, the gates to the other world would be shut.

On the other side of these gates lies the spirit world or other dimensions. Gatekeepers are in constant communication with beings who live there, who have the ability to teach us how to deal with ritual. And gatekeepers have the capacity to take other people to those places.

A gatekeeper's knowledge is different from the knowledge of mentors and elders. This is because elders do not necessarily have access to all the gateways. The gatekeepers, on the other hand, have access to all the dimensions. They can open any gate. Although their knowledge is very broad, elders will call upon gatekeepers to help them open a particular gate or help them better understand what the spirit world is about.

Gays and lesbians in the West are often very spiritual, but they have been taken away from their connection with spirit. My feeling is that without that outlet or that role in the culture, they have to find other ways of defining themselves. This could be one of the reasons why they would want to get married or make themselves look as though they do not have a unique purpose.

I have seen people in the West who have lost their identity try to usurp the role of gatekeeper once they learn about the power it involves. They do this for their own benefit, without really knowing what it means to be a true gatekeeper. Being a false gatekeeper is not helpful to anyone. It can only be harmful to the usurper.

These people need to understand that in the village a person doesn't become a gatekeeper out of a desire for power or even because of sexual orientation. No. Gatekeeping is part of one's life purpose, announced before birth and developed through rigorous initiatory training to ensure that its power is not misused. A gatekeeper is responsible for a whole village, a whole tribe. Gatekeeping is not a game.

Even though, in the village, homosexual relationships are not commonly the subject of ritual, here in the West they have become so, simply because of the circumstances of life. The ash rituals, and almost any other rituals I have described, may be used to strengthen gay relationships.

What we have looked at regarding intimacy, sexuality, ritual, conflict, and loss applies also to homosexual relationships in the West. Because any kind of relationship, unless it's false or empty or superficial, comes with problems. And there is a need to carefully maintain and sometimes repair it. Maybe the only difference for gays and lesbians would be to have other gatekeepers, in addition to nongay family members and friends, involved in their rituals.

CHAPTER 14

BARKA

I want to thank every reader for taking time to commune with the sacred. This is not a trivial subject; therefore it cannot be exhausted in a small book. Your response to this book, to the call of its subject, is proof that you feel deeply the crisis in which intimacy has been thrown and the necessity of bringing to it a radical healing.

For those who are interested in a spirited intimacy, listen more to the ancestors, to spirit, to the trees, to the animals. Focus on ritual. Listen to all those forces that come and speak to us that we usually ignore.

Somehow what I've said here is ringing a bell; what brought you to this book is that bell. You didn't pick up this book because you saw a crowd lined up for it. This is a sign that something in you is not dead. It's deliberately alive and expects to remain alive! That is something to celebrate. People may say that you're weird, that you are reading about weird people, but you know, perhaps it is time to celebrate being weird.

Barka. That means "Thank you."

SOBONFU SOMÉ, whose name means "keeper of ritual," was born and raised in Burkina Faso, the former Upper Volta. She is an initiated member of the Dagara tribe of West Africa. Sobonfu and her husband, Malidoma Somé, teach the ancient wisdom of their tribe throughout the world.

The Somés are involved in an ongoing project to provide water to the Dagara villages of Burkina Faso. Drilling equipment, pumps, and other materials are needed. Financial contributions and other services will help these efforts to continue. If you would like to receive information about the Somés' workshops, or about the Friends of the Dagara water project, please contact:

Echoes of the Ancestors
P.O. Box 4918
Oakland, CA 94605-6918
E-mail: Malidoma@earthlink.net
Internet: www.PrimaSounds.com/echoes/